THE
~WORLD~
VEGETARIAN
COOKBOOK

Designed by Philip Clucas MSIAD

Photographed by Peter Barry

Edited by Jillian Stewart

5121 The World Vegetarian Cookbook
Copyright © 1999 Quadrillion Publishing Ltd

This edition published in 1999 by
Colour Library Direct,
Godalming Business Centre,
Woolsack Way, Godalming,
Surrey, GU7 1XW

ISBN 1-84100-142-2

Printed and bound in Dubai

THE
~WORLD~
VEGETARIAN
COOKBOOK

Colour
Library
Direct

CONTENTS

CONTENTS

Introduction

It's official, vegetarianism is on the increase. Over the last few decades, a revolution in eating habits has taken place that has seen the number of vegetarians in both the United States and Great Britain rise enormously. Contrary to what many people believe, however, the vegetarian diet is not a recent phenomenon. Its current popularity may be a product of today's concern with the damage we are inflicting on our planet and the creatures we share it with, but it is by no means a late development, and certainly not one limited to the Western hemisphere.

Scientific evidence suggests that our early ancestors existed on a diet that consisted mainly of seeds, roots and berries – a diet typical of modern-day primates – and were compelled to become hunters only as a result of environmental changes which reduced this food supply. Conventional images of the resulting hunter-gatherer societies, however, overemphasise the importance of hunting, which in truth only provided the occasional meal to supplement the plant food gathered on a daily basis. The development of horticulture, which allowed people to stay in one place and invest the effort once expended on looking for food on growing it instead, allowed humankind to rely on a diet wholly based on plant foods. Poverty was obviously one reason for the reliance on such a diet, but over the centuries the most overwhelming reason has been a religious one. The ancient religions of the East and sections of the Buddhist and Hindu faiths, for instance, consider all animal life to be sacred, and followers therefore abstain from eating any flesh. This is no outmoded custom, however. Today, in India, around 70 per cent of the population are vegetarian for religious reasons. Sectors of the Christian church also adopted vegetarianism and played a vital role in the early beginnings of the movement on both sides of the Atlantic. Also, despite the declining part religion plays in our everyday lives in the West, it has undoubtedly influenced many of the ethical and moral questions raised by our highly-intensive system of meat production.

Whereas many people in the developing world are vegetarian for reasons of poverty or religion, the vast majority of those adopting a vegetarian diet in the West do so for very different reasons. To those who take a global view, one of the most compelling reasons is the sheer inefficiency of intensive meat production in a world where many go hungry – the huge swathes of land needed for beef production could be given over to crops, which are less ruinous to the environment and make vastly more efficient use of the land. More personal and less difficult than the complexities of world hunger and food supply is the concern for animal welfare. Many people are rightly worried by the way animals are raised and slaughtered, and they refrain from eating meat out of compassion. As if these reasons were not compelling enough, over recent years a meat-free diet has been shown to have substantial health benefits, including a reduced risk of high blood pressure, heart disease, cancer and diabetes. And these are just the most widely publicised health benefits; there are many others.

In a society whose diet has for centuries been dominated by meat, it is all too easy to forget that a large percentage of the world's inhabitants have a diet that consists largely of vegetable foods. This fact is also disguised by the tendency of foreign restaurants to ignore authentic recipes and tailor their menus to perceived Western tastes by adding meat. This gives a misleading picture of some of our favourite cuisines, and it comes as a surprise to many to discover just how suitable many authentic styles of cooking are for vegetarians. Notable among these are Chinese, Indian and Mediterranean, which all feature numerous exciting and delicious meat-free recipes.

Yet these are just a few of the styles of cooking that you will find within these pages. Drawing on a myriad recipes from places as far flung as Cuba, North Africa, Eastern Europe and Thailand, we take you on a culinary tour that highlights some of the world's best and most well-known vegetarian recipes – as well as many with which you will be unfamiliar.

The joy of exploring vegetarian cooking from around the world would once have been limited to the lucky and hardy few who travelled far afield. Today, however, we are in the enviable position of having a vast array of ingredients from around the world at our disposal. The most visible result of this are the rows of colourful and exotic fruits and vegetables in our supermarkets; but fresh produce is just part of the story – sun-dried tomatoes, harissa and balsamic vinegar are just a few of the exciting flavours to become popular recently, and they are just as valuable to the vegetarian cook as any other. This extraordinarily diverse array of foods offers the cook a unique opportunity to sample the best vegetarian recipes from around the world. Dishes that up until very recently would have been impossible to reproduce outside their country of origin, can now be created in your own kitchen.

The recipes that follow give a taste of some of the world's best vegetarian cooking. Simply turn the pages and you will find yourself on a culinary journey that will provide inspiration for years to come.

APPETISERS & SNACKS

As the introduction to a meal, an appetiser plays a vital role in enlivening the tastebuds and setting the style for the meal to follow. The varied recipes in this chapter have been chosen not only for their quality, but also to ensure a smooth transition to the featured main courses. Green Pepper and Avocado Dip, for instance, is the perfect introduction to a Mexican-themed meal, while Artichauts Aioli provides an impressive prelude to European recipes. Mixing and matching styles is also great fun, so why not try Asian Salad and then jump continents to the Americas for your main course. Also included in this chapter are a number of snacks, including favourites such as Falafel, and Spinach and Cheese Pie, as well as unusual dishes such as Imam Bayildi. What they all have in common, however, is an evocative and delicious flavour.

Makes 18 Samosas

Vegetable Samosas

AS A LARGE PROPORTION OF INDIA'S POPULATION IS VEGETARIAN, IT IS HARDLY
SURPRISING THAT THE ORIGINAL RECIPE FOR SAMOSAS IS A VEGETARIAN ONE.

Ingredients

Pastry

225g/8oz plain flour

60g/2oz butter

½ tsp salt

75ml/2½ fl oz warm water

Filling

450g/1lb potatoes

2 tbsps cooking oil

½ tsp black or white mustard seeds

1 tsp cumin seeds

2 dried red chillies,
coarsely chopped

1 onion, finely chopped

1-2 fresh green chillies, coarsely
chopped and seeded if a mild
flavour is preferred

½ tsp ground turmeric

1 tsp ground coriander

1 tsp ground cumin

1 tsp salt or to taste

1 tbsp chopped fresh
coriander leaves

1. Boil the potatoes in their skins while preparing the pastry.

2. To make the pastry, add the butter and salt to the flour and rub in well. Mix to a soft dough with the water. Knead until the dough feels soft and velvety.

3. Divide the pastry into 9 balls. Rotate each ball between your palms, then press it down to make a flat cake. Roll each cake into a 10cm/4-inch circles and cut into two. Use each semicircle of pastry as one envelope. Set aside while preparing the filling.

4. When the potatoes are cooked, allow them to cool, then peel and dice them. Set aside.

5. Heat the oil in a large frying pan and add the mustard seeds. As soon as they start crackling, add the cumin seeds, red chillies, onion and green chillies. Fry until the onions are soft. Add the turmeric, ground coriander and cumin. Stir quickly, then add the potatoes and salt. Reduce heat to low, stir and cook until the potatoes are thoroughly mixed with the spices.

6. Remove from the heat and stir in the coriander leaves. Cool thoroughly before filling the samosas. To fill the samosas, moisten the straight edge of the pastry with a little warm water, fold in half to make a triangular cone and press the edges together firmly.

7. Fill the cones with the filling, leaving about a 0.5cm/¼-inch border at the top. Moisten the top edges and press together well. Deep-fry the samosas over gentle heat until they are golden brown. Drain on kitchen paper and serve.

TIME Preparation takes about 60 minutes and cooking also takes about 60 minutes.

Serves 4

Imam Bayildi

THE NAME OF THIS TURKISH DISH MEANS THE IMAM OR PRIEST HAS FAINTED.
APPARENTLY THE DISH WAS SO DELICIOUS THAT HE PASSED OUT WITH PLEASURE.

Ingredients

2 large aubergines

150ml/5 fl oz olive oil

2 onions, finely chopped

2 cloves garlic, crushed

250g/9oz tomatoes, peeled
and chopped

½ tsp allspice

Juice of ½ lemon

1 tsp brown sugar

1 tbsp chopped fresh parsley

1 tbsp pinenuts

Salt and freshly ground
black pepper

1. Cut the aubergines in half lengthways and scoop out the flesh, leaving a substantial shell so they do not disintegrate when cooked.

2. Heat half the oil in a saucepan, add the onion and garlic, and fry until the onion has just softened. Add the aubergine flesh, tomatoes, allspice, lemon juice, sugar, parsley, pinenuts and salt and pepper. Simmer for about 20 minutes until the mixture has thickened.

3. Spoon the filling into the aubergine halves. Place the filled halves side by side in a greased ovenproof dish.

4. Mix the remaining oil with 140ml/¼ pint water and a little salt and pepper. Pour around the aubergines and bake in a preheated 180°C/350°F/Gas mark 4 oven for 30 to 40 minutes, or until completely tender.

TIME Preparation takes 25 minutes and cooking takes 1 hour.

SERVING IDEA Serve hot or cold garnished with fresh herbs and accompanied by chunks of wholemeal bread. If serving cold, chill for at least 2 hours before serving.

Serves 4

Tomato and Mozzarella

THE CLASSIC ITALIAN SUMMER APPETISER. USE LARGE, JUICY TOMATOES, FRESH
BASIL, MOIST MOZZARELLA AND THE FINEST OLIVE OIL YOU CAN BUY.

Ingredients

4 large tomatoes

*4 small packets round mozzarella
cheese*

10 fresh basil leaves

1 tbsp white wine vinegar

3 tbsps extra-virgin olive oil

*Salt and freshly ground
black pepper*

1. Cut the mozzarella cheese into round slices. Then, using a pastry cutter, trim the rounds into neat circles.

2. Turn the tomatoes on their sides and cut into neat slices. Discard the small outer slices. Alternate the tomato and mozzarella slices on the serving plates to make an attractive circle.

3. Cut the basil leaves lengthways into thin strips and mix into the vinegar and olive oil. Season the dressing to taste with salt and pepper and pour over the salad before serving.

TIME Preparation takes about 15 minutes.

COOK'S TIP Use a sharp, finely serrated knife to cut the cheese. Do not push down hard, but use a sawing action; this will keep the slices in one piece.

Tomatoes *Tomatoes have a fascinating history. They originated in South America (the word tomato is derived from an ancient Mexican word,* tomatl)*, with Peru in particular thought to be one of the earliest countries to cultivate it. The popularity of the tomato spread as a result of Spanish and Portuguese explorers returning to Europe with the plant. Initially it was more popular in southern Europe, hence its widespread use around the Mediterranean.*

Serves 4

Cheese and Vine Leaves

IN THIS GREEK RECIPE THE CHEESE IS COOKED OVER COALS TO GIVE
EXTRA FLAVOUR, BUT IT CAN ALSO BE GENTLY GRILLED.

Ingredients

*4 large pieces goat's, feta,
or haloumi cheese*

225ml/8 fl oz olive oil

*4 tbsps chopped fresh herbs
such as basil, tarragon,
oregano, marjoram
and parsley*

1 bay leaf

2 cloves garlic, crushed

Squeeze of lemon juice

To serve

*4 fresh vine leaves, washed,
or 4 brine-packed leaves,
soaked 30 minutes*

1 head radicchio

*Handful frisée or oak leaf lettuce
leaves, washed and torn into
bite-sized pieces*

1. If using goat's cheese, make sure it is not too ripe. Lightly score the surface of whichever cheese is used. Mix together the oil, herbs, garlic and lemon juice.

2. Place the cheese in a small, deep bowl and pour over the oil mixture. If cheese is not completely covered, pour on more oil. Cover and leave in the refrigerator overnight.

3. Drain the cheese and place in a hinged wire rack. Grill the cheese over hot coals, turning occasionally, until light golden brown and just beginning to melt.

4. Drain and dry the vine leaves, reserving the oil. Wash the radicchio and separate the leaves. Arrange the radicchio and frisée leaves on 4 small plates and place a vine leaf on top. Place the cooked cheese on top of the vine leaf and spoon some of the oil mixture over each serving.

TIME Overnight soaking is required for the cheese. Cooking takes 4 to 5 minutes.

Serves 3 – 4

Aubergine Slices in Yogurt

VARIATIONS OF THIS DELICIOUS INDIAN RECIPE CAN BE FOUND IN
MANY OTHER AREAS, PARTICULARLY TURKEY AND NORTH AFRICA.

Ingredients

1 tsp chilli powder

½ tsp ground turmeric

1 large aubergine, cut into
1cm/½-inch-thick round slices

Vegetable or olive oil for
deep frying

280ml/½ pint natural yogurt

1 tsp garam masala

¼ tsp salt

1 green chilli, seeded
and chopped

1 tsp chopped fresh
coriander leaves

1. Rub the chilli and turmeric powders into the aubergine slices.

2. Heat the oil in a large pan and deep-fry the aubergine slices, a few at a time, for 2 to 3 minutes. Drain the slices on kitchen paper.

3. Beat the yogurt and add the garam masala, salt, green chilli and fresh coriander. Mix well.

4. Arrange the aubergine slices on a serving platter or on individual dishes and pour the yogurt over.

VARIATION For a Middle Eastern flavour, leave out the chilli powder, turmeric and garam masala, and instead rub the aubergine with a little garlic and replace the fresh coriander with mint.

TIME Preparation takes 10 minutes and cooking 10 to 15 minutes.

Coriander This aromatic herb is a member of the parsley family, although its taste is very different from that of its more common relative. Fresh coriander can be grown easily and quickly, and is widely used in Asian cooking (with the exception of Japanese cuisine). In India, it is often stirred through a curry just before serving to add extra flavour, whereas in China it is more commonly used as a garnish.

Serves 4

Spinach-stuffed Mushrooms

MUSHROOMS ARE HIGHLY REGARDED IN MANY EUROPEAN COUNTRIES
WHERE THE AGE-OLD TRADITION OF MUSHROOM GATHERING HAS SURVIVED.

Ingredients

4 large or 8 medium flat
mushrooms, stalks discarded

60g/2oz butter

4 cloves garlic, crushed

2 onions, finely chopped

½ tsp nutmeg

1 tbsp olive oil

225g/8oz spinach, trimmed,
cooked and finely chopped

2 tbsps fresh white breadcrumbs

Salt and freshly ground
black pepper

1 egg, beaten

1 tbsp chopped fresh parsley
to garnish

1. Heat the butter in a frying pan. Add garlic, onion and nutmeg, and fry gently until the onion has softened. Remove from the pan and set aside to cool.

2. Heat the oil in another pan and sauté the mushrooms on both sides until lightly browned. Place underside-up in a shallow, ovenproof dish. Mix together the onion mixture, spinach, breadcrumbs and salt and pepper to taste. Stir in the beaten egg.

3. Cover each mushroom cap with the mixture, shaping neatly. Cover with aluminium foil and bake in a preheated 200°F/400°F/Gas mark 6 oven for 10 minutes. Serve immediately, garnished with chopped parsley.

TIME Preparation takes 15 minutes and cooking takes 20 minutes.

Mushrooms *It is estimated that there are thousands of edible varieties of mushroom in existence around the world, only a small percentage of which are harvested. The common mushroom is the most widely available in the West, although unusual varieties such as ceps and morels are becoming more widely available, as is the delicious range of Oriental mushrooms, in particular shittakes.*

Serves 4

Green Pepper and Avocado Dip

THAT FAVOURITE MEXICAN SNACK GUACAMOLE IS EXPANDED UPON IN THIS RECIPE.
MEXICAN AVOCADOS ARE GENERALLY REGARDED AS THE BEST, SO LOOK OUT FOR THEM.

Ingredients

*2 green peppers,
halved and cored*

*½ small fresh green chilli,
finely chopped*

1 small avocado

2 garlic cloves, crushed

3 spring onions, chopped

*Finely grated rind and juice
of 1 lime*

*4 tbsps chopped fresh
coriander leaves*

*Salt and freshly ground
black pepper*

*4 small wheat tortillas,
to serve*

*Lime wedge and a sprig of
fresh coriander to garnish*

TIME Preparation takes about
20 minutes and cooking takes 10 minutes.

1. Place the peppers, cut sides downward, on a grill pan. Grill under very high heat for about 10 minutes, until blackened. Peel off the skin and discard. Chop the flesh.

2. Place the chopped peppers and the remaining ingredients in a food processor or blender. Purée until smooth. Check the seasoning and add more lime juice if necessary.

3. Spoon into a serving bowl, then cover and chill. Garnish with lime and coriander just before serving. Serve with the tortillas and chunks of crisp, raw vegetables.

Green Peppers *The capsicum family, to which
the pepper belongs, originated in South America, but was widely
used in various areas of the American continent before it
eventually spread to Europe. The green pepper is an unripe
pepper which will turn red if left to ripen.*

Serves 6-12

Spinach and Cheese Pie

TRADITIONALLY MADE AT EASTER, THIS CLASSIC GREEK PIE IS NOW ENJOYED
ALL YEAR ROUND. IT IS PERFECT FOR SERVING AS PART OF A BUFFET.

Ingredients

450g/1lb pack filo pastry

900g/2lbs fresh spinach

3 tbsps olive oil

2 onions, finely chopped

3 tbsps chopped fresh dill

3 eggs, lightly beaten

Salt and freshly ground
black pepper

225g/8oz feta cheese, crumbled

120g/4oz butter, melted

1. Unfold the pastry on a flat surface and cut it to fit a large shallow baking dish. Keep the pastry covered.

2. Tear the stalks off the spinach, wash the leaves well and shred them with a sharp knife.

3. Heat the oil in a large saucepan, add the onion and cook until soft. Add the spinach and stir over a medium heat for about 5 minutes. Turn up the heat to evaporate any moisture.

4. Allow the spinach and onion to cool, then mix in the dill, eggs, salt, pepper and cheese.

5. Brush some of the melted butter on the bottom and sides of the baking dish. Brush the top sheet of filo pastry and place it in the dish. Brush another sheet and place that on top of the first. Repeat to make 8 layers of pastry.

6. Spread the filling over the layers in the bottom of the dish and cover with another 6 or 7 layers of pastry, brushing each layer with melted butter. Brush the top layer well and score the pastry in square or diamond shapes. Do not cut right through the pastry.

7. Sprinkle the top of the pie with water and bake in a preheated 190°C/375°F/ Gas mark 5 oven for 40 minutes, or until crisp and golden.

8. Leave the pie to stand for about 10 minutes and then cut through to the bottom layer. Lift out the pieces to a serving dish.

PREPARATION The pie can be cooked in advance and reheated for 10 minutes to serve hot.

TIME Preparation takes about 25 minutes and cooking takes about 40 minutes.

Serves 8

Indonesian-style Stuffed Peppers

FOR THIS ADAPTABLE RECIPE YOU CAN SUBSTITUTE PINENUTS
OR PEANUTS FOR THE CASHEWS.

Ingredients

2 tbsps olive oil

1 onion, chopped

1 clove garlic, crushed

2 tsps turmeric

1 tsp crushed coriander seeds

2 tbsps desiccated coconut

120g/4oz mushrooms, chopped

90g/3oz bulgur wheat

60g/2oz raisins

280ml/½ pint stock or water

2-3 tomatoes, peeled and chopped

60g/2oz cashew nuts

4 small green peppers, cored
and cut in half lengthways

2 tsps lemon juice

Vegetable stock for cooking

1. Heat the oil in a large saucepan, add
   the onion and garlic, and fry until
   lightly browned.

2. Add the turmeric, coriander and
   coconut, and cook gently for about
   2 minutes. Add the mushrooms and
   bulgur wheat, and cook for another
   2 minutes.

3. Add the raisins, water and tomatoes,
   and simmer gently for 15 to 20 minutes
   until the bulgur wheat is cooked.

4. Meanwhile, toast the cashew nuts in a
   dry frying pan until golden brown and
   blanch the peppers in boiling water for
   3 minutes.

5. Mix the nuts and lemon juice with the
   rest of the ingredients and fill the
   peppers with the mixture. Place the
   filled pepper halves in a large ovenproof
   dish and pour vegetable stock around
   them. Cook in a preheated 180°C/
   350°F/Gas mark 4 oven for 20 minutes.

TIME Preparation takes 20 minutes and
cooking takes about 45 minutes.

Serves 8

Falafel

THE NATIONAL DISH OF BOTH ISRAEL AND EGYPT, FALAFEL IS A COARSE
PASTE OF SPICED CHICKPEAS SHAPED INTO SMALL PIECES AND DEEP-FRIED.

Ingredients

*200g/7oz chickpeas, soaked
overnight in water*

*1 slice white bread, crust
removed*

2 cloves garlic, crushed

2 tbsps chopped fresh parsley

*60g/2oz bulgur wheat, rinsed
and drained*

½ tsp ground coriander

½ tsp ground cumin

½ tsp cayenne pepper

1 tsp salt

Oil for deep frying

TIME Preparation takes about
1 hour, plus overnight soaking
for the beans. Cooking takes
10 to 15 minutes.

1. Drain the chickpeas and rinse in fresh water. Grind them in a food processor or blender, putting them through twice if necessary to make a coarse paste.

2. Soak the bread in water, then squeeze it dry by hand. Chop the bread and mix with the crushed garlic and parsley. Add this mixture to the chickpeas. Add the bulgur, spices and salt, and mix well. Leave in the refrigerator for 30 minutes.

3. In a deep-fat fryer, preferably with a frying basket, heat the oil to very hot, about 180°C/350°F, or until a cube of bread will brown in 60 seconds. Wet your hands and shape the mixture into small balls about the size of a walnut.

4. Deep-fry the balls a few at a time for 2 to 3 minutes or until golden. Remove with a draining spoon and drain on kitchen paper. Serve immediately with mixed salad. Falafel are best when eaten very fresh. Do not store.

SERVING IDEA Falafel is eaten as a snack, packed in pita bread with plenty of lettuce, tomato and cucumber. It is generally accompanied by a hot sauce containing fenugreek, a bitter herb. An alternative sauce can be made by mixing Tabasco, or similar pepper sauce, with tomato sauce.

VARIATION Substitute canned chickpeas for the dried variety, but ensure you rinse them well before use.

Serves 4

Asian Salad

THE DEMANDS OF EVER MORE ADVENTUROUS CONSUMERS MEAN THAT MANY STORES
NOW STOCK THE SORT OF EXOTIC LEAVES USED IN THIS EASTERN RECIPE.

Ingredients

280g/10oz mixed young Asian
greens such as mustard greens,
bok choy, tatsoi and mizuna

⅓ head Chinese leaves,
shredded

90g/3oz mange tout, trimmed
and thinly sliced diagonally

60g/2oz chestnut mushrooms,
very thinly sliced

2 spring onions, cut lengthways
into 2.5cm/1-inch strips

120g/4oz cold boiled rice

1 tsp toasted sesame seeds,
to garnish

Dressing

280ml/½ pint vegetable stock

2 tbsps finely chopped red onion

½ tsp finely chopped fresh
root ginger

½ tsp chopped lemon grass

3 sprigs flat-leafed parsley

1 tbsp lime juice

½ tsp salt

2 tsps sesame seeds, toasted
and crushed

½ tsp sugar

1 tsp soy sauce

1 tsp sesame oil

1. First prepare the dressing. Place the stock, onion, ginger, lemon grass, parsley, lime juice and salt in a small saucepan. Bring to the boil, simmer for 5 minutes until reduced, then strain. Place 6 tbsps of the liquid in a blender with the crushed sesame seeds, sugar, soy sauce and sesame oil, and blend.

2. Tear the greens and bok choy stalks into bite-sized pieces.

3. Arrange all the greens and vegetables attractively on individual serving plates with a small mound of rice in the centre.

4. Spoon the dressing over the top and sprinkle with the sesame seeds.

TIME Preparation takes 15 minutes.

Spring Onions *The spring onion is simply an onion that has been picked very young, before it has had a chance to form a bulb. It has an ancient history and is known to have existed in Central Asia long before the start of the Christian era. Today, there are a large number of varieties, many of which are only used in their area of origin.*

Serves 4

Orange, Grapefruit and Mint Salad

FROM THE HEALTH-CONSCIOUS WEST COAST OF
AMERICA COMES THE PERFECT LOW-CALORIE APPETISER.

Ingredients

2 grapefruits

3 oranges

Liquid sweetener to taste
(optional)

8 sprigs of mint

TIME Preparation takes about
20 minutes, plus chilling time.

1. Using a serrated knife, cut away the peel and pith from the grapefruit and oranges. Carefully cut inside the skin of each segment to remove each section of flesh.

2. Squeeze the membranes over a bowl to extract all the juice. Sweeten the juice with the liquid sweetener, if required.

3. Arrange the orange and grapefruit segments alternately on 4 individual serving dishes.

4. Using a sharp knife, chop 4 sprigs of the mint very finely. Stir the chopped mint into the fruit juice.

5. Carefully spoon the juice over the arranged fruit segments and chill thoroughly. Garnish with a sprig of mint before serving.

PREPARATION Make sure all the pith is removed from the fruit, as it produces a bitter flavour.

VARIATION Use ruby grapefruits and blood oranges, when available, in place of the common types of fruit.

Serves 4

Artichauts Aioli

GARLIC MAYONNAISE MAKES THE PERFECT SAUCE FOR
ARTICHOKES IN THIS TYPICALLY PROVENÇAL APPETISER.

Ingredients

4 globe artichokes

1 slice lemon

1 bay leaf

Pinch of salt

Sauce aioli

2 egg yolks

2 cloves garlic, crushed

*Salt and freshly ground
black pepper*

280ml/½ pint olive oil

Lemon juice to taste

Chervil leaves to garnish

TIME Preparation takes
30 minutes and cooking takes
about 35 minutes.

1. To prepare the artichokes, break off the stems and twist to remove any tough fibres. Trim the base so that the artichokes will stand upright. Trim the points from all the leaves and wash the artichokes well.

2. Bring a large pan of water to the boil with the slice of lemon and bay leaf. Add a pinch of salt and, when the water is boiling, add the artichokes. Simmer for 35 minutes over a moderate heat. While the artichokes are cooking, prepare the sauce.

3. Beat the egg yolks and garlic with a pinch of salt and pepper in a deep bowl, or in a food processor or blender. Add the olive oil, a few drops at a time, while whisking by hand, or in a thin, steady stream with the machine running. If preparing the sauce by hand, once half the oil is added, the remainder may be added in a thin, steady stream. Add lemon juice when the sauce becomes very thick. When all the oil has been added, adjust the seasoning and add more lemon juice to taste.

4. When the artichokes are cooked, the bottom leaves will pull away easily. Remove them from the water with a draining spoon and drain upside down on kitchen paper or in a colander. Allow to cool and serve with the sauce aioli. Garnish with a sprig of chervil.

Serves 4

Hummus

THIS AUTHENTIC MIDDLE EASTERN SNACK
HAS GAINED WIDESPREAD POPULARITY.

Ingredients

225g/8oz cooked or tinned
chickpeas (reserve liquid)

4 tbsps light tahini (sesame paste)

Juice of 2 lemons

90ml/3 fl oz olive oil

3-4 cloves garlic, crushed

Salt to taste

1. Put the chickpeas in a food processor or blender together with 140ml/¼ pint of the reserved cooking liquid or can juices.

2. Add the tahini, lemon juice, half of the olive oil, garlic and salt. Blend until smooth, adding a little more liquid if it is too thick.

3. Leave to stand for an hour or so to let the flavours develop. Serve with the remaining olive oil drizzled over the top.

TIME Preparation takes 10 minutes, standing time is 1 hour.

Artichoke *The globe artichoke is the flower bud of a member of the thistle family. In addition to its delicious flavour and unusual texture, the globe artichoke has valuable nutritional qualities, including diuretic and purgative properties, and a significant amount of vitamin C, folic acid and iron. Small artichoke heads, which are picked at the end of season, can often be found preserved in olive oil.*

Left: Artichauts Aioli

Serves 6

Burritos

THE NAME OF THIS TEX-MEX RECIPE MEANS 'LITTLE DONKEYS'.
BEANS ARE THE TRADITIONAL FILLING IN THIS POPULAR DISH.

Ingredients

6 tortillas (see page 124)

1 tbsp oil

1 onion, chopped

450g/1lb tin refried beans

6 lettuce leaves, shredded

120g/4oz Cheddar cheese, grated

2 tomatoes, sliced

2 tbsps snipped chives

140ml/¼ pint soured cream

Chopped fresh coriander leaves

Taco sauce

1 tbsp oil

1 onion, diced

1 green pepper, cored and diced

1 red or green chilli

½ tsp ground cumin

½ tsp ground coriander

½ clove garlic, crushed

Pinch of salt, freshly ground
black pepper and sugar

400g/14oz tin tomatoes

Tomato purée (optional)

1. Wrap the tortillas in foil and heat in a warm oven to soften.

2. Heat the oil in a large frying pan, add the onion and cook until soft but not coloured. Add the beans and heat through.

3. Spoon the mixture down the centre of each tortilla. Top with lettuce, cheese, tomatoes and chives. Fold over the sides to form a long rectangular parcel. Make sure the filling is completely enclosed.

4. Place burritos in an ovenproof dish, cover and cook in a preheated 180°C/350°F/Gas mark 4 oven for about 20 minutes.

5. Meanwhile, make the taco sauce. Heat the oil in a heavy-based saucepan and, when hot, add the onion and pepper. Cook slowly to soften slightly.

6. Chop the chilli and add with the cumin, coriander and garlic. Cook for 2 to 3 minutes, then add the seasoning, sugar and tomatoes with their juice. Break up the tomatoes with a fork or potato masher.

7. Cook for another 5 to 6 minutes over moderate heat to reduce and thicken slightly. Add tomato purée for colour, if necessary.

8. Spoon the taco sauce over the cooked burritos. Top with soured cream and sprinkle with chopped coriander to serve.

TIME Preparation takes about 25 minutes, not including making the tortillas. Cooking takes about 30 minutes.

PREPARATION Heat just before serving as Burritos do not reheat well.

SERVING IDEA Serve with a crisp green salad.

Serves 6–8

Gazpacho

THIS TYPICALLY SPANISH SOUP IS THE PERFECT SUMMER FIRST COURSE. THE RECIPE COMES FROM ANDALUSIA, IN SOUTHERN SPAIN.

Ingredients

1 green pepper, cored and chopped

8 tomatoes, peeled, seeded and chopped

1 large cucumber, peeled and chopped

1 large onion, chopped

90-150g/3-5oz French bread, crusts removed

3 tbsps red wine vinegar

840ml/1½ pints water

Pinch of salt and freshly ground black pepper

2 cloves garlic, crushed

3 tbsps olive oil

2 tsps tomato purée (optional)

Garnish

1 small onion, diced

½ small cucumber, diced

3 tomatoes, peeled, seeded and diced

½ green pepper, cored and diced

1. Combine the prepared vegetables in a deep bowl and add the bread, breaking it into small pieces by hand. Mix together thoroughly.

2. Add the vinegar, water, salt, pepper and garlic. Pour the mixture, a third at a time, into a food processor or blender and purée for about 1 minute, or until the soup is smooth.

3. Pour the purée into a clean bowl and gradually beat in the olive oil using a whisk. Add enough tomato purée for a good red colour.

4. Cover the bowl tightly and refrigerate for at least 2 hours, or until thoroughly chilled. Before serving, beat the soup to ensure all the ingredients are blended, and then pour into a large chilled soup tureen or into chilled individual soup bowls. Serve the garnishes in separate bowls for guests to help themselves.

VARIATION Use only enough garlic to suit your own taste, or omit it altogether. Vary the garnishing ingredients by using croûtons, chopped spring onions, red onions and red or yellow peppers.

TIME Preparation takes about 20 minutes, plus at least 2 hours chilling.

FRESH SALADS

The popularity of salads is booming. The vast array of exciting and colourful ingredients that now find their way into our supermarkets from the four corners of the world is at times astonishing. In this chapter you will find inspiration for turning those raw ingredients into delicious and innovative dishes. Ranging from the simple, but stunning, Roast Pepper and Basil Salad from the Mediterranean to the unusual Papaya and Bean Sprout Salad from the Orient, this section has a diverse range of dishes designed to appeal to all tastes.

Some of the best classic dishes are also featured, including the ultimate French salad, Mesclun, and that most valued of Middle Eastern salads, Tabouleh.

Serves 4

Roast Pepper and Basil Salad

FOR THOSE WHO DO NOT LIKE THE AGGRESSIVE TASTE OF RAW PEPPERS, THIS ITALIAN SALAD IS A REVELATION. GRILLING THEM ADDS A WONDERFUL SMOKY, MELLOW TASTE.

Ingredients

4 yellow peppers, cored and cut in half

4 red peppers, cored and cut in half

1 tbsp extra-virgin olive oil

1 tbsp red wine vinegar

Bunch of fresh basil

TIME Preparation and cooking take about 20 minutes.

SERVING IDEA Serve as a first course, or with another salad as a complete meal.

1. Preheat the grill. Place the pepper halves on the grill pan and grill under high heat. The peppers can also be grilled over a gas flame or barbecue. They will take 2 to 3 minutes to cook.

2. When the skin is wrinkled and blackened in places, quickly transfer the peppers to a large plastic bag and fold the top over. Leave them in the bag to cool.

3. The skin should now peel off very easily. Slice the peppers into narrow strips.

4. Arrange the strips on a flat serving platter and sprinkle with the oil and vinegar. Scatter basil leaves over the peppers and leave to marinate for an hour or so at room temperature. Do not chill, but eat at room temperature.

Serves 4 – 6

Curried Chickpea and Rice Salad

A BLEND OF AROMATIC SPICES BRINGS AN EXOTIC FLAVOUR TO THIS RICE SALAD. SERVE WITH FRESH MULTIGRAIN BREAD ROLLS AND MIXED SALAD LEAVES.

Ingredients

225g/8oz mixed brown and wild rice

1 tsp olive oil

1 clove garlic, crushed

1 tsp ground coriander

1 tsp ground cumin

1 tsp turmeric

½ tsp hot chilli powder

140ml/¼ pint passata

2 tbsps red wine vinegar

1 tbsp tomato ketchup

Salt and freshly ground black pepper

180g/6oz broccoli florets

3 tbsps finely chopped fresh parsley

1 tbsp chopped fresh thyme

2 bunches spring onions, chopped

2 x 400g/14oz tins chickpeas, rinsed and drained

180g/6oz sultanas

1. Cook the rice in a large pan of lightly salted, boiling water for about 20 minutes, or according to the packet instructions, until the rice is cooked and just tender. Drain thoroughly and keep hot.

2. Meanwhile, make the dressing. Heat the oil in a saucepan, add the garlic and spices, and cook gently for 2 minutes, stirring.

3. Add the passata, vinegar, tomato ketchup and seasoning, and mix well.

Heat gently, stirring occasionally, until the mixture comes to the boil. Reduce the heat and keep the dressing warm.

4. Cook the broccoli in a pan of lightly salted, boiling water for about 5 minutes, until just tender. Drain thoroughly.

5. Place the cooked rice in a bowl, add the spicy tomato dressing and stir to mix. Add the cooked broccoli and the remaining ingredients and toss together to mix. Serve the rice salad warm or cold.

TIME Preparation takes 15 minutes and cooking takes 20 minutes.

Garlic *Valued for centuries in the East as a basic seasoning, garlic has become extremely popular in Britain over recent years. Supermarkets tend to stock only one type of garlic, although there are many types, ranging from small white bulbs to the large purple-tinged heads and the round, bulb-like garlic from China.*

Mesclun

THIS VARIATION ON A MEDIEVAL FRENCH SALAD
FEATURES AN EXCITING MIXTURE OF SALAD LEAVES.

Ingredients

*Choose from a combination
of these ingredients:*

Leaves

Frisée

Lamb's lettuce

Radicchio

Rocket plant

Chicory

Cos lettuce

Oak leaf lettuce

Escarole

Round-heart lettuce

Watercress

Herbs

Lovage

Basil

Chives

Chervil

Tarragon

Marjoram

Edible marigold petals

Nasturtium buds and flowers

1. Wash your chosen leaves in cold water and dry, either with kitchen paper or a clean tea towel.

2. Mix the leaves together and add your chosen mix of herbs. Sprinkle your favourite dressing over the salad.

TIME Preparation takes about 10 minutes.

VARIATION Spike your favourite dressing with a crushed clove of garlic and a little grainy mustard, crushed papaya seeds, or capers.

Salad Greens

The variety of cultivated greens now available makes it easier than ever to produce the mix of flavours required for a mesclun. Lettuce has been cultivated since very early times and was undoubtedly known to the Greeks and Romans, although there were far fewer forms than are cultivated today.

Left: Mesclun

Serves 4

Tofu Salad

THIS THAI SALAD CAN ALSO BE SERVED HOT. SIMPLY RETURN THE TOFU TO THE WOK, HEAT THROUGH AND SERVE IMMEDIATELY.

Ingredients

90ml/3 fl oz oil

225g/8oz cubed tofu

2 cloves garlic, crushed

120g/4oz broccoli florets

120g/4oz mange tout

1 tbsp soy sauce

1 tsp salted black beans

½ tsp palm sugar

90ml/3 fl oz vegetable stock

½ tsp cornflour

VARIATION Use smoked tofu for a different flavour.

1. Heat the oil in a wok and fry the tofu until golden on all sides. Remove with a slotted spoon, set aside to cool, then refrigerate until required.

2. Pour off most of the oil from the wok. Add the garlic and fry until softened. Stir in the broccoli and mange tout, and stir-fry until just tender.

3. Add the soy sauce, black beans and sugar, and fry for 1 minute.

4. Mix a little of the stock with the cornflour, return this to the remaining stock, then add this to the wok. Cook until the sauce thickens slightly.

5. Transfer to a serving dish and chill until required. To serve, scatter the tofu cubes over the cooked vegetables.

TIME Preparation takes 15 minutes and cooking takes about 10 minutes.

Serves 4

Carrot Salad with Sesame Dressing

THE CARROTS IN THIS MIDDLE EASTERN DISH ARE COATED
WITH TAHINI, A DELICIOUS SESAME SEED PASTE.

Ingredients

4 large carrots

120g/4oz raisins

120g/4oz chopped walnuts

2 tbsps sesame seeds

Dressing

2 tbsps oil

1 tbsp lemon juice

6 tbsps tahini (sesame paste)

90ml/3 fl oz warm water

2 tbsps double cream

Salt and freshly ground
black pepper

1 tbsp sugar

1. Place the carrots in iced water for 1 hour. Dry them and grate coarsely into a bowl. Add the raisins, walnuts and sesame seeds.

2. Mix the dressing ingredients together thoroughly, adding more cream if the dressing appears too thick. If the dressing separates, beat vigorously until it comes together before adding additional cream.

3. Toss with the carrot salad and serve.

TIME Preparation takes about 1 hour.

Nuts *A valuable source of protein, nuts have always played an important part in the vegetarian diet. They are now imported from many areas of the world, but some of the most healthy are familiar ones such as peanuts and walnuts. Thought to be native to central Asia and south-west Europe, the walnut is also widely grown in California.*

Serves 4

Rice and Nut Salad

THIS REFRESHING SALAD IS HIGH IN PROTEIN FROM THE RICE,
NUTS AND BEANS, AND VERY LOW IN SATURATED FATS.

Ingredients

2 tbsps olive oil

2 tbsps lemon juice

Salt and freshly ground
black pepper

120g/4oz sultanas

60g/2oz currants

280g/10oz cooked brown rice,
well drained

90g/3oz blanched almonds,
chopped

60g/2oz cashew nuts,
chopped

60g/2oz shelled walnuts,
chopped

420g/15oz tin peach slices in
natural juice, drained
and chopped

¼ cucumber, cubed

120g/4oz cooked red kidney
beans

1 tbsp chopped, pitted
black olives

1. Put the olive oil, lemon juice and salt and pepper into a screw-top jar and shake vigorously until the ingredients have combined.

2. Put the sultanas and currants into a small bowl and cover with boiling water. Leave to stand for 10 minutes, then drain the fruit.

3. Mix together the rice, nuts, soaked fruit, peaches, cucumber, kidney beans and olives in a large mixing bowl.

4. Pour the dressing over the salad and mix together thoroughly, ensuring all the ingredients are evenly coated.

TIME Preparation takes about 15 minutes.

SERVING IDEA Serve the salad on a bed of crisp lettuce.

Serves 4

Pink Grapefruit, Avocado and Walnuts with Mixed Leaves

THIS CALIFORNIAN-STYLE SALAD IS A LIGHT AND REFRESHING COMBINATION OF CONTRASTING TEXTURES AND FLAVOURS.

Ingredients

1 large red-fleshed grapefruit

1 large avocado

Lemon juice

60g/2oz baby spinach leaves, coarsely shredded

3-4 handfuls frisée lettuce, torn into bite-sized pieces

Small handful of watercress or lamb's lettuce

4 radishes, sliced diagonally

30g/1oz walnut halves

Extra-virgin olive oil

Salt and freshly ground black pepper

Walnut oil

1. Using a very sharp knife, cut a horizontal slice from the top and the bottom of the grapefruit. Remove the remaining peel and the pith by cutting downward following the contours of the fruit. Working over a bowl, cut down between the flesh and membrane of each segment. Ease out the flesh and put it in a bowl. Cut the segments in half crossways and set aside with the juice.

2. Cut the avocado in half lengthways then slice crossways. Sprinkle with lemon juice.

3. Toss the salad greens with a few drops of olive oil – just enough to barely coat the leaves. Season with salt and freshly ground black pepper. Arrange on individual plates and scatter with the radishes and walnut halves. Add the avocado and grapefruit segments. Sprinkle with the grapefruit juice and just a little dash of the walnut oil. Serve immediately.

TIME Preparation takes 15 minutes.

AVOCADO *The avocado originated in South America, where it has been grown for thousands of years. In contrast, it was virtually unknown in Europe until the second half of the 20th century, when it was introduced by the Israelis. Although it is often said to be high in fat compared to other fruits, it contains monounsaturated fat – the same type so valued in olive oil!*

Serves 4

Black-eyed Bean and Orange Salad

THIS FRENCH-STYLE SALAD HAS A FRESH TASTE THAT IS GIVEN
A DELICIOUS PEPPERY 'BITE' BY THE ADDITION OF WATERCRESS.

Ingredients

225g/8oz black-eyed beans, soaked

1 bay leaf

1 slice of onion

Juice and grated rind of 1 orange

75ml/5 tbsps olive oil

6 black olives, pitted and quartered

4 spring onions, trimmed and chopped

2 tbsps each chopped fresh parsley and basil

Salt and freshly ground black pepper

4 whole oranges

1 bunch watercress, washed

1. Place the beans, bay leaf and onion slice in a saucepan and add enough water to cover by 2.5cm/1 inch. Bring to the boil and boil rapidly for 10 minutes. Reduce the heat and simmer gently for about 50 minutes to 1 hour, until the beans are tender. Drain well.

2. Put the orange juice, rind and oil in a large bowl and whisk together with a fork. Stir in the olives, spring onions and chopped herbs.

3. Add the cooked beans to the dressing and season with salt and pepper. Mix thoroughly to coat the beans well.

4. Peel and segment the oranges; chop the segments of 3 of the oranges and add to the beans.

5. Arrange the watercress on individual serving plates and pile equal amounts of the bean and orange salad on to this. Arrange the remaining orange segments on the plate and serve immediately.

SERVING IDEA Serve in split wholemeal pita bread, or in taco shells.

TIME Preparation takes about 20 minutes, plus soaking. Cooking takes about 1 hour.

Serves 4

Sweet and Sour Mixed Bean Salad

BEANS PROVIDE PROTEIN, FOLIC ACID, IRON AND POTASSIUM, AND VIRTUALLY NO FAT — ALL
OF WHICH MAKES THEM PERFECT VEGETARIAN FARE.

Dressing

3 tbsps olive oil

3 tbsps unsweetened apple juice

2 tbsps red wine vinegar

2 tbsps clear honey

2 tbsps light soy sauce

2 tbsps tomato ketchup

2 tbsps medium sherry

1 clove garlic, crushed

1 tsp ground ginger

Salt and freshly ground
black pepper

Ingredients

180g/6oz green beans,
trimmed and halved

1 small red onion, sliced

1 small red pepper,
cored and diced

1 small yellow pepper,
cored and diced

120g/4oz raisins

400g/14oz tin chickpeas,
rinsed and drained

200g/7oz tin sweetcorn, drained

400g/14oz tin red kidney beans,
rinsed and drained

2-3 tbsps finely chopped
fresh parsley

1. Steam the green beans over a pan of simmering water for about 10 minutes, until just tender. Drain and rinse under cold water to cool them. Drain well.

2. Place the cooled green beans, onion, peppers, raisins, chickpeas, corn, kidney beans and parsley in a large bowl and mix together.

3. Place all the dressing ingredients in a small bowl or blender and whisk together until thoroughly mixed. Pour over the mixed beans and toss together to mix.

TIME Preparation takes 20 minutes and cooking takes 10 minutes.

SERVING IDEA Serve the mixed bean salad with crusty French bread, or toasted pita pockets.

Beans *Beans, like potatoes, originated in the American continent and were introduced into Europe by returning explorers. The beans that we are all familiar with – red kidney and haricot, for instance – are shell beans, as opposed to the pod beans that are picked before the bean has a chance to develop fully. There is a huge variety of beans now on the market, although the flavour difference between many of these is slight.*

Serves 6

Mixed Tomato and Pepper Salad with Parsley Dressing

A FRESH AND COLOURFUL MEDITERRANEAN SALAD.

Ingredients

4 red plum tomatoes

4 yellow tomatoes

225g/8oz cherry tomatoes

1 red pepper, cored and
sliced into rings

1 yellow pepper, cored and
sliced into rings

1 large red onion, sliced
into rings

4 sun-dried tomatoes, soaked,
drained and finely chopped

Dressing

90ml/3 fl oz natural yogurt

60ml/2 fl oz mayonnaise

2 tsps wholegrain mustard

3-4 tbsps chopped fresh parsley

Salt and finely ground
black pepper

Fresh parsley sprigs to garnish

1. Slice the plum and yellow tomatoes thinly and halve the cherry tomatoes.

2. Place the tomatoes, peppers and onion slices in a serving bowl or on a serving platter, and toss together to mix. Scatter the sun-dried tomatoes over the top.

3. Place the yogurt, mayonnaise, mustard, parsley and salt and pepper in a small bowl, and mix thoroughly.

4. Sprinkle the dressing over the tomato and pepper salad and toss lightly to mix. Garnish with fresh parsley sprigs before serving.

TIME Preparation takes 15 minutes.

VARIATION Use standard red tomatoes if yellow ones are not available.

*Right: Mixed Tomato and Pepper
Salad with Parsley Dressing*

Serves 6

Moroccan Potato Salad

THIS DELICATELY SPICED POTATO SALAD IS A
GOOD ALTERNATIVE TO THE OFTEN RATHER BLAND
POTATO SALADS OF THE WEST.

Ingredients

900g/2lbs small new
potatoes, washed

3 tbsps tomato juice

½ tsp ground cumin

½ tsp ground paprika

½ tsp ground coriander

2½ tsps ground turmeric

½ tsp ground cinnamon

½ tsp ground ginger

1 clove garlic, crushed
(optional)

2 bunches spring onions,
chopped

1 yellow pepper, cored
and diced

2-3 tbsps chopped
fresh coriander

75ml/5 tbsps mayonnaise

75ml/5 tbsps natural yogurt

Salt and freshly ground
black pepper

1. Cook the potatoes in a large saucepan of lightly salted, boiling water for 10 to 15 minutes, until cooked and tender. Drain thoroughly and allow to cool completely.

2. Place the tomato juice, spices and garlic, if using, in a small saucepan and cook gently for 2 minutes, stirring. Allow to cool slightly.

3. Place the cold potatoes in a large bowl, add the spring onions, yellow pepper and coriander, and stir to mix.

4. Place the mayonnaise, yogurt, spice mixture and seasoning in a small bowl, and mix together thoroughly. Pour the dressing over the potatoes and toss together to mix.

5. Cover and set aside for 30 minutes before serving. Alternatively, cover and chill in the refrigerator until ready to use.

TIME Preparation takes 20 minutes and cooking takes 20 minutes.

VARIATION This salad may be served warm. Toss the warm cooked potatoes with the dressing and serve.

Serves 4

Tricolour Pasta Salad

THIS SALAD LOOKS ABSOLUTELY STUNNING WITH ITS COLOURS OF THE
ITALIAN FLAG. IT IS A FILLING DISH, SUITABLE AS A SUMMER ENTRÉE.

Ingredients

*550g/1¼lbs pasta spirals
(or other pasta shapes)*

5 sun-dried tomatoes in oil

*150g/5 fl oz vinaigrette dressing
(made with 3 parts virgin
olive oil to 1 part wine vinegar
or lemon juice, plus salt,
pepper and a pinch of
mustard powder)*

5 stems fresh marjoram

3 stems fresh basil

225g/8oz mozzarella cheese, cubed

120g/4oz black olives, pitted

1. Cook the pasta in plenty of boiling water until al dente – about 12 minutes. Drain the pasta and rinse in plenty of cold water to keep the shapes separate and stop it cooking further. Transfer to a large mixing bowl.

2. Cut the sun-dried tomatoes into small strips. Mix the dressing ingredients, shaking them in a bottle, or blending them in a blender.

3. Snip or finely chop the marjoram and basil. Combine the cooled pasta with the cheese, olives and tomatoes. Add enough dressing to lightly coat the pasta, then add the herbs. Stir well and leave at room temperature, lightly covered, for about 1 hour, for the flavours to combine. Serve at room temperature.

TIME Preparation and cooking take 20 minutes.

SERVING IDEA Serve with Italian breads and a green salad.

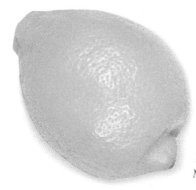

Lemon *The original home of the lemon is thought to be southeastern Asia. From there it gradually came west, until in about AD 1000 the Arabs introduced it into the Mediterranean region. To begin with it was only used medicinally, but gradually its culinary importance took precedence. Today, lemons are grown widely in the Mediterranean region, as well as in the United States.*

Serves 4

Warm Salad with Avocado, Grapes, Blue Cheese and Walnuts

WARM SALADS ARE POPULAR IN FRANCE. THEY ARE UNDOUBTEDLY DELICIOUS, BUT BEWARE — THEY MUST BE SERVED IMMEDIATELY TO PREVENT THE LEAFY INGREDIENTS GOING LIMP.

Ingredients

Mixed salad leaves, such as frisée, radicchio, lamb's lettuce, or watercress

2 avocados, peeled and sliced

180g/6oz black grapes, halved and pitted

4 tbsps chopped fresh mixed herbs

120g/4oz walnut pieces

120g/4oz diced or crumbled blue cheese

3 tbsps mixed walnut oil and grapeseed oil

2 tbsps lemon vinegar

Pinch of sugar

1. Tear the salad leaves into small pieces and place in a large bowl. If using lamb's lettuce, separate the leaves and leave whole. Remove any tough stalks from the watercress.

2. Add the avocado slices to the salad leaves, along with the grapes, chopped herbs, walnuts and cheese.

3. Put the oils, vinegar and sugar into a screw-top jar and shake vigorously until the dressing is well blended.

4. Pour the dressing into a frying pan and heat until bubbling. Remove from the heat, add to the prepared salad and toss, taking care not to break up the avocado pieces. Serve immediately.

TIME Preparation takes about 15 minutes and cooking takes 2 to 3 minutes.

Grapes *Vines are thought to predate mankind's existence and grapes were probably one of the first fruits to be seriously cultivated. The best-known product associated with grapes is of course wine, but they are also widely valued as a fruit, either fresh or dried.*

Serves 4–6

Bavarian Potato Salad

IT IS BEST TO PREPARE THIS SALAD A FEW HOURS IN ADVANCE
TO ALLOW THE POTATOES TO ABSORB THE FLAVOURS.

Ingredients

900g/2lbs tiny new potatoes

4 tbsps olive oil

4 spring onions, finely chopped

1 clove garlic, crushed

2 tbsps chopped fresh dill
or 1 tbsp dried

2 tbsps wine vinegar

½ tsp sugar

Salt and freshly ground
black pepper

2 tbsps chopped fresh
parsley

1. Wash the unpeeled potatoes, put them in a pan, cover with water and boil until just tender.

2. While the potatoes are cooking, heat the olive oil in a frying pan, add the spring onions and garlic, and fry for 2 to 3 minutes until they have softened a little. Add the dill and cook gently for another minute.

3. Add the wine vinegar and sugar, and stir until the sugar dissolves. Remove from the heat and add a little salt and pepper.

4. Drain the potatoes and pour the dressing over them while they are still hot. Allow to cool and sprinkle with the chopped parsley before serving.

TIME Preparation takes 15 minutes and cooking takes 15 minutes.

Sugar Most widely known as a sweetening agent in desserts, sugar is also valuable for sweetening and balancing the flavour of some savoury dishes. Most of the world's refined sugar is derived from sugar cane, a native of the Orient which spread first to the Mediterranean, and then to the American continent in the 16th century.

Tabouleh

THIS IS A TRADITIONAL SALAD FROM THE MIDDLE EAST. THE MAIN INGREDIENT IS BULGUR WHEAT, WHICH IS PARTIALLY COOKED, CRACKED WHEAT.

Ingredients

180-200g/6-7oz bulgur wheat

1 tsp salt

340ml/12 fl oz boiling water

450g/1lb tomatoes, chopped

½ cucumber, diced

3-4 spring onions

Dressing

60ml/2 fl oz olive oil

60ml/2 fl oz lemon juice

2 tbsps chopped fresh mint

4 tbsps chopped fresh parsley

2 cloves garlic, crushed

1. Mix the bulgur wheat with the salt, pour over the boiling water and leave to stand for 15 to 20 minutes. All the water will then be absorbed.

2. Mix together the ingredients for the dressing and pour over the soaked bulgur. Fold in lightly with a spoon.

3. Leave for two hours or overnight in a refrigerator or cool place.

4. Add the tomatoes, cucumber and spring onions. Mix together and serve.

COOK'S TIP A few cooked beans can be added to make this dish more substantial.

TIME Preparation takes about 20 minutes; standing time is about 2 hours.

Serves 4

Goat Cheese Salad with Tarragon

THIS MEDITERRANEAN SALAD IS SIMPLICITY ITSELF TO PREPARE. THE FRESH HERBS
AND OLIVE OIL GIVE IT A LOVELY FLAVOUR REDOLENT OF SULTRY SUMMER DAYS.

Ingredients

12 small slices white bread

4 small goat cheeses
(not too fresh)

4 small servings of mixed green
salad, washed and dried

1 tbsp chopped fresh tarragon

1 tbsp tarragon vinegar

2 tbsps olive oil

Salt and freshly ground
black pepper

TIME Preparation takes about 25 minutes and cooking takes 5 minutes.

1. Using a pastry cutter, cut the sliced bread into 12 neat circles.

2. Cut each cheese horizontally into 3 circles the same size as the bread and place on the prepared bread. Sprinkle the chopped tarragon over the cheese.

3. To prepare the dressing, mix together the tarragon vinegar, olive oil and salt and pepper. Stir or shake well and pour over the prepared mixed green salad.

4. Place the cheese and bread rounds into a moderately hot oven and cook until the cheese melts slightly and the top is golden.

5. Remove from the oven and place the cheese and toast circles on top of the tossed salad.

Serves 4 – 6

Oriental Salad

THIS NUTRITIOUS SALAD CONTAINS TOFU. A STAPLE FOOD IN MUCH
OF ASIA, TOFU IS VENERATED FOR ITS HEALTH-GIVING PROPERTIES.

Ingredients

1 cake tofu, cut into small cubes

140ml/¼ pint vegetable oil

120g/4oz mange tout, ends trimmed

60g/2oz mushrooms, sliced

60g/2oz broccoli florets

2 carrots, thinly sliced

2 celery sticks, thinly sliced

4 spring onions, thinly sliced

60g/2oz unsalted roasted peanuts

120g/4oz bean sprouts

½ head Chinese leaves,
shredded

Dressing

3 tbsps lemon juice

2 tsps honey

1 tsp grated fresh root ginger

3 tbsps soy sauce

Dash of sesame oil

1. Drain the tofu well and press gently to
remove excess moisture. Cut into
1cm/½-inch cubes.

2. Heat 2 tbsps of the vegetable oil in a
wok or frying pan (save the remaining
oil for the dressing).

3. Add the mange tout, mushrooms,
broccoli, carrots and celery, and cook
for 2 minutes. Remove the vegetables
and set them aside to cool.

4. When cool, mix the cooked vegetables
with the onions, peanuts and bean
sprouts. Mix the dressing ingredients
together and pour over the vegetables.
Add the tofu and toss carefully.

5. Arrange a bed of Chinese leaves on a
serving dish and pile the salad
ingredients on top to serve.

TIME Preparation takes 25 minutes and
cooking takes 2 minutes.

Mange Tout *These young pea pods, picked before the
peas have matured, have a fresh, crunchy flavour. They are
commonly used in two very different styles of cooking –
French and Chinese. Where others disdain the humble pea,
the French have always treated it with the respect it deserves
and have done much to champion mange tout. In Chinese cooking,
mange tout is valued for its crunchy texture in stir-fries.*

Serves 6

Curried Rice Salad

ALTHOUGH INFLUENCED BY INDIAN COOKING, THIS RECIPE IS UNDOUBTEDLY
AN AMALGAM OF VARIOUS STYLES. IT IS DELICIOUS NONETHELESS.

Ingredients

180g/6oz long-grain rice

1 tbsp curry powder

4 spring onions, trimmed
and sliced

2 celery sticks, sliced

1 green pepper, cored and diced

10 black olives, halved and pitted

60g/2oz sultanas

4 tbsps toasted, slivered almonds

4 tbsps desiccated coconut

2 hard-boiled eggs, chopped

Dressing

140ml/¼ pint mayonnaise

1 tbsp mango chutney

Juice and grated rind of ½ lime

4 tbsps natural yogurt

Salt

Garnish

2 avocados, peeled and cut
into cubes

Juice of ½ lime or lemon

1. Cook the rice in boiling, salted water for about 12 minutes, or until tender. During the last 3 minutes of cooking time, drain away half the water and stir in the curry powder. Leave to continue cooking over a gentle heat until the rice is cooked and the water has evaporated.

2. Allow to stand, covered, for about 5 minutes. Toss the rice with a fork, drain away any excess water and leave to cool.

3. Combine the rice with the remaining salad ingredients, stirring carefully so that the eggs do not break up.

4. Mix the dressing ingredients together thoroughly. Chop any large pieces of mango in the chutney finely. Stir the dressing into the salad and toss gently to coat.

5. Arrange the rice salad in a mound on a serving dish. Sprinkle the cubed avocado with the lemon juice to keep it green and place around the rice salad before serving.

TIME Preparation takes 20 minutes and cooking takes about 12 minutes.

Limes *The lime is thought to be native to southern Asia and was introduced to the Middle East and the Mediterranean by the Arabs in the 10th century. Today, they are cultivated all over the subtropical world, with the West Indies and Mexico being the world's principal suppliers.*

Serves 4

Greek Salad

A GREAT FAVOURITE THAT HAS THE ADDED
ADVANTAGE OF BEING EASY TO PREPARE.

Ingredients

2 tomatoes

½ green pepper, cored and
coarsely chopped

¼ cucumber, coarsely chopped

2 celery sticks, finely sliced

1 tsp finely chopped fresh basil

Few crisp lettuce leaves

120g/4oz diced feta cheese

16 black olives, pitted

Dressing

4 tbsps olive oil

2 tbsps lemon juice

1 clove garlic, crushed

Large pinch of oregano

Salt and freshly ground
black pepper

1. Cut each tomato into eight pieces and place in a large mixing bowl. Add the pepper, cucumber, celery and chopped basil.

2. Mix together the oil, lemon juice, garlic, oregano, salt and pepper, and pour over the salad. Mix well to coat all the vegetables.

3. Arrange a few leaves of lettuce in the bottom of a serving bowl and pile the salad on the top, followed by the cheese cubes. Garnish with the olives.

TIME Preparation takes 15 minutes.

L e t t u c e *This invaluable salad ingredient has been grown for thousands of years, first by the Chinese and later by the Greeks and Romans, who did much to spread its use throughout Europe. In contrast to the way it is commonly served today, during the Middle Ages lettuce was braised and served hot.*

Serves 2

Papaya and Bean Sprout Salad

BEAN SPROUTS AND PAPAYA ADD A TASTE OF THE ORIENT
TO THIS REFRESHING SALAD.

Ingredients

1 large, ripe papaya

Squeeze of lime juice

*200g/7oz (about 4 handfuls)
green and red salad leaves
such as frisée, romaine, lamb's
lettuce and oak leaf lettuce, torn
into bite-sized pieces*

*15g/½ oz (small handful)
rocket*

*½ small cucumber, very
thinly sliced*

120g/4oz bean sprouts

Citrus dressing

¼ tsp Dijon mustard

1 tsp olive oil

1½ tbsps orange juice

1½ tbsps fresh lime juice

Pinch of sugar

*Salt and freshly ground
black pepper to taste*

TIME Preparation takes
15 minutes.

1. Halve the papaya lengthways and scoop
   out the seeds, reserving a few for
   garnish. Using a small, sharp knife,
   carefully remove the skin. Slice the flesh
   lengthways into thin segments. Place in
   a shallow dish and sprinkle with a
   squeeze of lime juice.

2. Arrange the leaves on individual plates.
   Scatter the cucumber, bean sprouts and
   papaya over the top and sprinkle with
   the reserved papaya seeds.

3. Purée the dressing ingredients in a
   blender and spoon over the salad. Serve
   at once with crackers or crusty bread.

Serves 6

Pasta and Vegetables in Parmesan Dressing

THIS WONDERFUL PASTA SALAD IS BOTH COLOURFUL AND DELICIOUS.

Ingredients

450g/1lb pasta spirals or
other shapes

225g/8oz assorted vegetables
such as:

Courgette, cut into rounds
or julienne strips

Broccoli, trimmed into very
small florets

Mange tout, ends trimmed

Carrots, cut into julienne

Celery, cut into julienne

Cucumber, cut into julienne

Spring onions, thinly shredded
or sliced

Asparagus tips

French beans, sliced

Red or yellow peppers,
cored and thinly sliced

Dressing

120ml/4 fl oz olive oil

3 tbsps lemon juice

1 tbsp chopped fresh parsley

1 tbsp chopped fresh basil

60g/2oz freshly grated
Parmesan cheese

2 tbsps mild mustard

Salt and freshly ground
black pepper

Pinch of sugar

1. Cook pasta in a large saucepan of boiling, salted water with 1 tbsp oil for 10 to 12 minutes, until just tender. Rinse under hot water to remove starch. Leave in cold water.

2. Simmer all the vegetables, except the cucumber, in boiling, salted water for about 3 minutes, until just tender. Rinse in cold water and leave to drain.

3. Mix the dressing ingredients together well.

4. Drain the pasta thoroughly and toss with the dressing. Add the vegetables and toss to coat.

TIME Preparation takes 25 minutes and cooking takes about 15 minutes.

Asparagus The asparagus sold in supermarkets is a cultivated variety of a type that can still be found growing wild around the Mediterranean and in western and central Asia. There are three main varieties of asparagus: white, purple and green. White asparagus is picked as soon as the spears of the plant appear through the soil, the purple is harvested when the shoots are a little higher, and the green when they are higher still.

Serves 4

Quinoa Salad

THIS LIGHT SALAD USES QUINOA, THE SOUTH
AMERICAN SEED THAT THE INCAS ONCE REFERRED TO
AS 'THE MOTHER GRAIN'. IT CONTAINS A HIGH
AMOUNT OF PROTEIN AND HAS A DELICATE, SLIGHTLY
NUTTY FLAVOUR.

Ingredients

180g/6oz quinoa

Seeds from 4 cardamom pods,
crushed

460ml/16 fl oz water

Salt

1 tsp tamari (Japanese soy sauce)

2 tsps olive oil

Freshly ground black pepper

90g/3oz mange tout, ends trimmed

150g/5oz black grapes,
halved and seeded

3 tbsps snipped chives

Radicchio and Little Gem
lettuce

TIME Preparation takes
20 minutes and cooking takes
15 minutes plus standing time.

VARIATION Use bulgur wheat
instead of quinoa.

1. Dry-fry the quinoa and cardamom
   seeds in a small saucepan for a minute
   or two, until the quinoa starts to colour.

2. Add the water and ½ tsp salt. Bring to
   the boil, cover and simmer over very
   low heat until the liquid is absorbed,
   about 15 minutes.

3. Remove from the heat, fluff up with a
   fork and stir in the lemon juice, tamari
   and olive oil. Transfer to a bowl and
   leave to cool.

4. Plunge the mange tout into boiling
   water for 30 seconds, then drain. Slice
   diagonally into three and stir into the
   quinoa.

5. Set aside a few grapes as a garnish and
   add the remainder to the quinoa. Stir in
   the chives and salt and pepper to taste.

6. When ready to serve, arrange the
   lettuce leaves around the edge of a
   shallow serving dish or individual plates
   and pile the quinoa salad on top.
   Garnish with the reserved grapes and
   serve with crackers.

Left: Quinoa Salad

Serves 4–6

Sweet and Sour Fruit Salad

DO NOT BE PUT OFF BY THE SAVOURY SEASONING IN THIS EXOTIC SALAD – IT GIVES THE DISH A DEFINITE EDGE. SERVE AS AN APPETISER, SIDE SALAD, OR SNACK.

Ingredients

2 bananas, peeled and sliced

1 large guava, chopped

1 pear, peeled and chopped

225-280g/8-10oz tinned peaches, drained and chopped

225-280g/8-10oz pineapple chunks

1 small, fresh papaya, peeled, seeded and cut into chunks

A few grapes, seeded

1 apple, peeled, cored and chopped

2 tsps lemon juice

Salt

¼ tsp freshly ground black pepper

¼ tsp chilli powder

Pinch of black rock salt (kala namak)

1. Put all the fruits into a large bowl. Sprinkle with lemon juice, salt, pepper and chilli. Mix well.

2. Add pinch of ground black rock salt. Mix and serve. Note: many other fruits may be added, such as mango, kiwi, plum, lychees and melon.

TIME Preparation takes 20 to 25 minutes.

Pears *The first pears were the small, green fruits of the wild pear tree, which can still be found growing all over Europe and as far east as the Himalayas. By Roman times, Pliny, that tireless compiler of botanical information, could list 38 varieties. Today, there are over 3,000, although only a few are cultivated widely.*

MAIN MEALS

The main course is usually the focal point of a meal and as such
it needs to be inspired, delicious and nutritious. Drawing on classic
and innovative recipes from around the world, this chapter fulfils
these criteria by embracing the lighter, brighter colours and textures
that are so popular today.

The inhabitants of many exotic countries have long understood how
to cook vegetables – stir-frying is a perfect example – and this is
reflected in their cuisines. With everything from classic Chinese
stir-fries to a Herbed Lentil Stew, Tunisian Couscous from the
Middle East, and Gado Gado from Indonesia, this chapter reflects
the diversity that makes vegetarian cooking across the world
so exciting.

Serves 4

Ten Varieties of Beauty

THE NUMBER 'TEN' REFERS TO THE SELECTION OF VEGETABLES IN THIS
EXOTIC CHINESE DISH, WHICH IS SIMPLICITY ITSELF TO MAKE.

Ingredients

10 dried shittake mushrooms

2 carrots

60ml/2 fl oz vegetable oil

3 celery sticks, trimmed and
sliced diagonally

90g/3oz mange tout, trimmed

8 baby corn cobs, halved
lengthways

1 red pepper, cored
and sliced

4 spring onions, sliced

60g/2oz bean sprouts

10 water chestnuts, sliced

60g/2oz tin sliced bamboo
shoots, drained

280ml/½ pint vegetable stock

2 tbsps cornflour

3 tbsps light soy sauce

1 tsp sesame oil

1. Place the mushrooms in a bowl and add boiling water to cover. Leave to stand for 30 minutes. Drain the mushrooms, and remove and discard the stalks.

2. Cut the carrots into ribbons using a potato peeler.

3. Heat the oil in a wok or large frying pan, add the celery, mange tout and baby corn, and fry for 3 minutes. Add the pepper and carrots, and stir-fry for 2 minutes.

4. Stir in the remaining vegetables and stir-fry for 3 to 4 minutes, until all the vegetables are cooked, but still crisp.

5. Add the stock to the pan. Combine the cornflour, soy sauce and sesame oil, and stir into the pan. Cook, stirring constantly, until the sauce thickens. Serve immediately.

TIME Preparation takes 15 minutes, plus soaking. Cooking takes about 15 minutes.

Serves 4

Chickpea and Pepper Casserole

CHICKPEAS ARE USED EXTENSIVELY IN MIDDLE EASTERN CUISINE. HERE, GROUND
CUMIN AND MINT GIVE THIS COLOURFUL CASSEROLE A REAL NORTH AFRICAN FLAVOUR.

Ingredients

225g/8oz chickpeas, soaked
overnight

2 tbsps vegetable oil

1 onion, sliced

1 clove garlic, crushed

1 green pepper, cored
and sliced

1 red pepper, cored
and sliced

½ tsp ground cumin

2 tsps chopped fresh parsley

1 tsp chopped fresh mint

4 medium tomatoes, seeded
and cut into strips

Salt and freshly ground
black pepper

TIME Preparation takes 20 minutes, plus
overnight soaking. Cooking takes about
3 hours.

1. Drain the chickpeas, then rinse and
place in a pan with enough water to
cover them by 2.5cm/1 inch. Bring to
the boil and boil rapidly for 10 minutes.
Reduce the heat and simmer gently for
about
2 hours, or until the chickpeas are soft.
Drain and reserve the liquid.

2. Heat the oil in a saucepan and fry the
onion, garlic and peppers for about
5 minutes. Stir in the cumin and fry
for 1 minute.

3. Make the reserved liquid up to 280ml/
½ pint and add to the pan with the
cooked beans.

4. Add all the remaining ingredients and
bring slowly to the boil. Cover and
simmer for 30 minutes. Adjust the
seasoning, if necessary, and serve.

Serves 4

Wholemeal Vegetable Quiche

QUICHES ARE A GREAT FAVOURITE IN BOTH BRITAIN AND FRANCE; THIS RECIPE
IS UNUSUAL IN THAT IT HAS A WHOLEMEAL CRUST.

Ingredients

180g/6oz wholemeal
plain flour

90g/3oz butter

About 2 tbsps cold water

2 tbsps oil

1 small red pepper,
cored and diced

120g/4oz courgettes, diced

2 spring onions, trimmed
and sliced

1 tomato, peeled, seeded
and chopped

2 eggs, beaten

140ml/¼ pint milk

Salt and freshly ground
black pepper

Tomato slices and chopped
fresh parsley to garnish

1. Place the flour in a bowl and rub in the butter until the mixture resembles fine breadcrumbs. Add enough cold water to mix to a firm dough, then roll out and use to line an 20cm/8-inch flan tin.

2. Line the dish with greaseproof paper and fill with baking beans. Bake for 15 minutes in a preheated 200°C/400°F/Gas mark 6 oven, removing the parchment and beans halfway through the cooking time.

3. Reduce the oven temperature to 180°C/350°F/Gas mark 4. Heat the oil in a pan and fry the pepper and courgette for 2 minutes. Add the spring onion and tomato, and fry for 1 minute. Spoon the vegetable mixture into the flan tin.

4. Beat the eggs and milk together and season well. Pour over the vegetables. Return to the oven and bake for 30 minutes, or until the filling is just set. Garnish with sliced tomatoes and chopped parsley.

TIME Preparation takes about 15 minutes and cooking takes about 50 minutes.

P e p p e r Both black and white peppercorns come from a vine of the Peperaceae family, which grows widely in southeast Asia. Black peppercorns come from the unripe berries, which are fermented and dried until they blacken and become hard. White pepper, in contrast, is made by sun-drying the inner seed of the peppercorn.

Mixed Vegetable Curry

IN THIS INDIAN CURRY, A VARIETY OF SEASONAL VEGETABLES ARE COOKED
TOGETHER IN A SAUCE FLAVOURED WITH GROUND SPICES, ONIONS AND TOMATOES.

Ingredients

4-5 tbsps vegetable oil

1 large onion, finely chopped

1cm/½-inch cube fresh root ginger, peeled and finely sliced

1 tsp ground turmeric

1 tsp ground coriander

1 tsp ground cumin

1 tsp paprika

4 small ripe tomatoes, peeled and chopped

225g/8oz potatoes, peeled and diced

90g/3oz sliced green beans

120g/4oz carrots, sliced

90g/3oz garden peas

450ml/15 fl oz warm water

2-4 whole fresh green chillies

1 tsp garam masala

1 tsp salt or to taste

1 tbsp chopped fresh coriander leaves

1. Heat the oil over medium heat, add the onion and fry until lightly browned, about 6 to 7 minutes.

2. Add the root ginger and fry for 30 seconds. Adjust heat to low and add the turmeric, coriander, cumin and paprika. Stir to mix well. Add half the tomatoes and fry for 2 minutes, stirring continuously.

3. Add the potatoes, green beans, carrots, peas and water. Stir well. Bring to the boil, cover and simmer until vegetables are tender, about 15 to 20 minutes.

4. Add the remaining tomatoes and the chillies. Cover and simmer for 5 to 6 minutes.

5. Add the garam masala and salt, and mix well. Stir in half the coriander leaves and remove from the heat. Put the curry into a serving dish and sprinkle the remaining coriander leaves on top.

COOK'S TIP Frozen peas and beans may be used for convenience, but the cooking time should be adjusted accordingly.

TIME Preparation takes 25 to 30 minutes and cooking takes 30 minutes.

Serves 6

Tunisian Couscous

COUSCOUS IS A TYPE OF FINE SEMOLINA MADE FROM WHEAT GRAIN. IT IS
STEAMED OVER A STEW WHICH IT IS THEN MIXED THROUGH.

Ingredients

840ml/1½ pints vegetable stock

1 onion, coarsely chopped

2 garlic cloves, crushed

1 tsp cumin seeds, toasted
and crushed

200g/7oz tin chopped tomatoes

4 carrots, quartered

1 small celeriac, cut into
2.5cm/1-inch pieces

4 potatoes, quartered

½ tsp harissa or chilli powder

½ tsp salt

¼ tsp freshly ground black pepper

280g/10oz couscous

3 courgettes, cut into thick slices

Chopped fresh coriander to garnish

1. Heat 90ml/3 fl oz of the stock in a large
   pan over which a steamer will fit. Add
   the onion to the pan and cook over
   medium heat until soft.

2. Add the garlic, cumin and tomatoes,
   and cook for 2 to 3 minutes, stirring.

3. Add the carrots, celeriac, potatoes,
   remaining stock, harissa or chilli, salt
   and pepper. Bring to the boil, cover and
   simmer for 20 minutes.

4. Soak the couscous in warm water for
   10 minutes. Drain thoroughly and put
   in a metal sieve or cheesecloth-lined
   steamer.

5. Add the courgettes to the vegetables,
   then fit the steamer over the pan,
   making sure the bottom does not touch
   the stew. Steam the couscous, covered,
   for 30 minutes, until heated through.

6. To serve, turn the couscous into a
   shallow serving dish and fluff with a
   fork. Moisten with a little stock from
   the vegetables. Using a slotted spoon,
   arrange the vegetables in the middle
   and garnish with coriander. Serve the
   remaining vegetable stock in a pitcher.

TIME Preparation takes 30 minutes and
cooking takes 50 minutes.

COOK'S TIP Ethnic stores sell couscous
and the special steamer in which to cook
it, known as a couscousière.

SERVING IDEA Serve the couscous with
pita bread and a bowl of natural yogurt
sprinkled with ground coriander and a
pinch of cayenne pepper.

Green Beans *These are simply the unripe pods of
a standard bean plant. It is thought the bean plant originated
in America and was introduced into Europe in the 16th century.
It was particularly popular in France, hence its alternative
name of French bean.*

Serves 4

Ravioli with Ricotta Cheese

MAKING YOUR OWN PASTA GIVES A REAL INSIGHT INTO WHY ITALIANS ENJOY
THE WHOLE PROCESS OF PREPARING AND EATING HOME-COOKED FOOD.

Ingredients

Filling

30g/1oz butter or margarine

1 egg yolk

225g/8oz ricotta cheese

60g/2oz Parmesan cheese, grated

2 tbsps chopped fresh parsley

Salt and freshly ground black pepper

Dough

250g/9oz strong plain flour

Pinch of salt

3 eggs

Tomato sauce

1 tbsp olive oil

30g/1oz bacon

1 small onion, chopped

1 bay leaf

1 tbsp chopped fresh basil

1 tbsp flour

400g/14oz tin chopped tomatoes

Salt and freshly ground black pepper

1 tbsp double cream

1. To make the filling, beat the butter to a cream, add the egg yolk and blend well. Beat the ricotta cheese to a cream and add the butter and egg mixture gradually, mixing until smooth. Add the Parmesan cheese, parsley and salt and pepper to taste. Set aside.

2. To make the dough, sieve the flour into a bowl with the salt. Make a well in the centre and add the eggs. Work the flour and eggs together with a spoon, then knead by hand until a smooth dough is formed. Leave to rest for 15 minutes.

3. Lightly flour a board and roll the dough out thinly into a rectangle. Cut the dough in half.

4. Shape the filling into small balls and set them about 3.5cm/1½ inches apart on one half of the dough. Place the other half on top and cut out the ravioli with a small pastry cutter. Seal the edges with a fork or your fingertips.

5. Cook the ravioli in batches in a large, wide pan with plenty of boiling, salted water until tender, about 8 minutes. Remove carefully with a slotted spoon.

6. While the pasta is boiling, prepare the sauce. Heat the oil, add the bacon and onion, and fry until golden. Add the bay leaf and basil, and stir in the flour. Cook for 1 minute, remove from the heat and add the tomatoes gradually, stirring continuously. Add salt and pepper to taste.

7. Return the pan to the heat and bring to the boil. Simmer for 5 minutes, remove the bay leaf and press the sauce through a sieve. Stir in the cream and adjust the seasoning.

8. Pour the sauce over the ravioli and serve immediately.

COOK'S TIP Always buy fresh Parmesan and grate it yourself as its flavour is far superior to that of ready-grated Parmesan.

TIME Preparation takes 30 minutes and cooking takes 20 minutes.

Serves 4

Daal Dumplings in Yogurt

TWO TYPES OF DAAL FEATURE IN THIS UNUSUAL AND DELICIOUS INDIAN RECIPE.
MOONG DAAL IS SIMILAR TO YELLOW SPLIT LENTILS, WHILE URID DAAL IS A WHITE LENTIL.

Ingredients

120g/4oz urid daal, washed and soaked for 1 hour

60g/2oz moong daal, washed and soaked for 1 hour

½ tsp salt

2.5cm/1-inch piece root ginger, peeled and finely chopped

2 green chillies, finely chopped

60g/2oz mixed raisins and sultanas

Vegetable or olive oil for deep frying

Yogurt sauce

450ml/¾ pint natural yogurt

¼ tsp salt

½ tsp cumin seeds

½ tsp coriander seeds

2 sprigs fresh coriander leaves, chopped for garnish

1. Blend the drained urid daal and moong daal with sufficient water in a food processor or blender to make a very thick purée. Put the purée into a mixing bowl and add salt, ginger, chillies and mixed fruits. Mix well.

2. Heat the oil and add small spoonfuls of the mixture to the hot oil to make small dumplings. (To make them more uniform, dampen your hands in water, and form a little of the mixture into a flat, round shape before lowering gently into the oil.) Fry for 6–8 minutes, or until golden brown, turning occasionally. Drain on kitchen paper. Make all the dumplings in the same way.

3. Soak the fried dumplings in water for 2 to 3 minutes. Gently squeeze out any excess water and arrange on a flat serving dish. Mix the yogurt and salt together and pour over the dumplings.

4. Dry roast the cumin and coriander seeds for 1 to 2 minutes in a frying pan. Place the roasted spices in folded kitchen paper and crush with a rolling pin to give a coarse powder.

5. Sprinkle the ground spice mixture over the yogurt and garnish with chopped fresh coriander. Alternatively, sprinkle with a pinch of paprika powder.

TIME Preparation takes 5 minutes and 1 hour for soaking. Cooking takes about 30 minutes.

Root Ginger *Originating in India, fresh root ginger is widely used in Oriental cooking. Having spread to Europe, ginger was then taken by the Spanish to the West Indies, from where its cultivation spread rapidly. As well as being used fresh, root ginger is also pickled (when it turns a light pink colour) and used as a garnish in China and Japan.*

Makes One Pizza

Roast Aubergine and Tomato Pizza

DESPITE ITS OVEREXPOSURE, PIZZA REMAINS A GREAT BOON FOR VEGETARIANS.
THIS RECIPE IS JUST THAT LITTLE BIT DIFFERENT.

Ingredients

Dough

225g/8oz plain flour

Pinch of salt

6g/¼oz sachet easy-blend
dried yeast

1 tbsp olive oil

180ml/6 fl oz warm water

Topping

90ml/3 fl oz passata

Olive oil

1 large aubergine,
cut into slices

Salt

2 beefsteak tomatoes, sliced

2 cloves garlic, sliced

Freshly ground black pepper

Fresh basil leaves

1. Sieve the flour and salt into a warm mixing bowl and stir in the yeast. Make a well in the centre and add the olive oil and enough water to mix to a soft dough (you may not need all the water).

2. Turn out onto a floured surface and knead for a few minutes, until the dough is soft but not sticky. Shape into a round ball and roll out to form a circle 25cm/10 inches in diameter.

3. Place the dough on a lightly oiled baking sheet and prick all over with a fork. Spread the base with the passata. Allow to stand in a warm place while preparing the topping.

4. Heat about 4 tbsps olive oil in a large frying pan and fry the aubergine slices on both sides until beginning to brown. You may need to do this in batches; add extra olive oil as required.

5. Arrange alternate slices of aubergine and tomato on top of the pizza. Sprinkle with garlic and season well. Tear the basil into pieces and scatter on top.

6. Drizzle with olive oil and bake in a preheated 200°C/400°F/Gas mark 6 oven for 25 to 30 minutes, or until the base is cooked and golden.

TIME Preparation takes about 30 minutes and cooking takes about 40 minutes.

Serves 4–6

Smoked Tofu Kedgeree with Almonds

TOFU IS EXTREMELY POPULAR IN THE FAR EAST, WHERE IT IS REGARDED AS HAVING ALMOST MAGICAL QUALITIES. HERE, IT IS VALUED FOR BEING LOW IN FAT AND HIGH IN PROTEIN.

Ingredients

200g/7oz long-grain brown rice

1 tsp salt

3 eggs

30g/1oz butter

1 tbsp grapeseed or safflower oil

1 cake smoked tofu, drained, pressed dry, and cut into 1.5cm/3/4-inch cubes

2 tbsps flaked almonds

5 tbsps chopped fresh parsley or chives

Salt and freshly ground black pepper

1. Rinse the rice and place it in a pan with the salt and enough water to cover by the depth of your thumb. Bring to the boil, cover tightly, and simmer over a very low heat for 30 to 40 minutes, until all the liquid is absorbed.

2. Meanwhile, put the eggs in a pan, cover with water and bring to the boil. Boil for 5 minutes exactly, then remove from the heat and drain. Remove the shells and coarsely chop the white and yolk.

3. Tip the rice into a warmed serving bowl, breaking up any lumps with a fork. Stir in the eggs and butter, and keep warm.

4. Heat the oil in a small pan and gently fry the tofu for a minute or two, until heated through. Add it to the rice and eggs. Fry the almonds until golden brown and add to the rice.

5. Stir in the parsley and a little more butter, if necessary. Season with salt and pepper, and serve.

TIME Preparation takes 20 minutes and cooking takes 40 minutes.

Parsley *In the past, parsley was used more as a medicinal herb than a culinary one. It is widely used today, however, as a flavouring and garnish for a wide range of dishes. The two most common types of parsley are the curly-leaved variety, which is often used to make sauces, and common parsley, whose flat leaves can be a little more subtle in flavour.*

Serves 4

Herbed Lentil Stew

THIS TYPICAL MIDDLE EASTERN STEW IS A HEARTY
AND HEALTHY MIX OF LENTILS, SPINACH AND
POTATOES, FLAVOURED WITH LEMON AND GARLIC.

Ingredients

450g/1lb red lentils

460ml/16 fl oz water

2 tbsps vegetable oil

1 large onion, sliced

2 garlic cloves, crushed

2 tbsps chopped fresh coriander

450g/1lb spinach, trimmed
and chopped

2 potatoes, peeled

Juice of 1 lemon

½ tsp salt

¼ tsp cayenne pepper

TIME Preparation takes
15 minutes and cooking takes
about 1½ hours.

1. Wash the lentils and pick over them to remove any small stones or other impurities. Put the lentils in a pan and add water. Bring to the boil over high heat, then reduce the heat, cover the pan and cook for 20 minutes.

2. Heat the oil in a large heavy-based pan. Add the onion and cook over medium heat until the onion is transparent, about 5 minutes.

3. Add the garlic and coriander, and cook 5 minutes more. Add the spinach and cook for another 5 minutes, stirring constantly.

4. Add the potatoes and lentils with their cooking liquid to the pan. Bring to the boil over a high heat, then reduce the heat, cover the pan, and simmer for 1 hour, or until thick. Add the lemon juice, salt and black pepper just before serving.

Moors and Christians

ORIGINALLY FROM CUBA, THE BLACK BEANS AND
WHITE RICE IN THIS RECIPE REPRESENT THE OPPOSING
FORCES WHEN THE SARACENS INVADED SPAIN.

Ingredients

225g/8oz black beans, soaked
overnight and cooked until soft

2 tbsps vegetable oil

1 onion, chopped

4 cloves garlic, crushed

1 green pepper, cored and
finely chopped

2 large tomatoes, peeled and
finely chopped

280g/10oz long-grain rice

Salt and freshly ground
black pepper

Little bean cooking water,
if required

1. Drain the cooked beans and mash
   3 tbsps to a paste with a fork, adding a
   little bean cooking water, if necessary.

2. Heat the oil in a large pan and fry the
   onion, garlic and pepper until soft.

3. Add the tomatoes and cook for
   2 minutes. Add the bean paste and stir.

4. Add the cooked beans, rice and enough
   water to cover. Bring to the boil, cover
   and simmer for 20 to 25 minutes, until
   the rice is just cooked. Serve hot.

TIME Preparation takes 15 minutes.
Cooking takes 1 to 1½ hours for the
beans and 25 minutes for the finished dish.

VARIATION A small tin of tomatoes
may be used in place of fresh ones.

Left: Moors and Christians

The World Vegetarian Cookbook 73

Serves 4

Mushroom and Herb Risotto

FRESH CHOPPED MIXED HERBS ADD A VIBRANT FLAVOUR TO THIS APPETISING
RISOTTO, WHICH IS IDEAL SERVED WITH FRESH CRUSTY BREAD AND A GREEN SALAD.

Ingredients

1 red onion, chopped

3 leeks, washed and thinly sliced

2 cloves garlic, crushed

1 red pepper, cored and diced

4 celery sticks, chopped

225g/8oz long-grain brown rice

225g/8oz button mushrooms, sliced

*225g/8oz chestnut
mushrooms, sliced*

570ml/1 pint vegetable stock

280ml/½ pint dry white wine

*Salt and freshly ground
black pepper*

200g/7oz tin sweetcorn, drained

120g/4oz frozen peas

*3-4 tbsps chopped fresh
mixed herbs*

*Fresh Parmesan cheese shavings
to taste*

Fresh herb sprigs to garnish

1. Place the onion, leek, garlic, pepper, celery, rice, mushrooms, stock, wine and seasoning in a large pan, and stir to mix.

2. Bring to the boil and simmer, uncovered, for 25 to 30 minutes, stirring occasionally, until almost all the liquid has been absorbed.

3. Stir in the sweetcorn and peas and cook gently for about 10 minutes, stirring occasionally.

4. Stir in the chopped herbs and stir again to mix. Serve sprinkled with Parmesan cheese shavings and fresh herb sprigs.

TIME Preparation takes 15 minutes
and cooking takes 45 minutes.

Red Onions *This variety of onion – used extensively in Asian and Mediterranean cooking – is becoming much more popular elsewhere. As well as an attractive colour, the red onion has a sweet flavour that makes it perfect for using raw or lightly cooked.*

Rice Pilaf with Dried Cranberries

WITH ITS FRUITY FLAVOURS, THIS BRIGHTLY COLOURED WILD AND BASMATI
RICE PILAF MAKES A BEAUTIFUL VEGETARIAN MAIN COURSE.

Ingredients

1 red onion, very finely chopped

280ml/½ pint vegetable stock

*3 tender celery sticks, leaves
included, finely sliced*

3 carrots, coarsely grated

*1 green chilli, seeded and finely
chopped*

*4 spring onions, green parts
included, thinly sliced*

90g/3oz dried cranberries

1 tbsp olive oil

500g/1lb 2oz cooked wild rice

225g/8oz cooked brown basmati rice

*Finely grated rind
of 1 small orange*

*Juice of 3 small oranges
(about 90ml/3 fl oz)*

1 tsp salt

*¼ tsp freshly ground
black pepper*

TIME Preparation takes
25 minutes, plus rice cooking
time. Cooking takes 10 minutes.

1. Place the onion and 6 tablespoons of the stock in a large nonstick frying pan. Cook for 3 to 4 minutes, until translucent.

2. Add the celery, carrots, chillies, green onions and cranberries. Cook over medium heat for 2 minutes, until the vegetables are just tender but still crisp and brightly coloured. Remove from the pan and set aside.

3. Add the oil to the pan over high heat. Stir in the rice and toss for 2 minutes to heat through. Lower the heat and stir in the grated orange rind, juice, remaining stock, salt and pepper. Simmer for 1 minute.

4. Return the vegetables to the pan and toss with the rice to heat through before serving.

5. Serve the pilaf with Indian bread or pita pockets and a bowl of natural yogurt.

Serves 4

Cabbage Parcels

STUFFED CABBAGE LEAVES ARE POPULAR IN MANY COUNTRIES, ESPECIALLY IN EASTERN EUROPE. A TASTY TOMATO SAUCE IS ONE OF THE BEST ACCOMPANIMENTS.

Ingredients

120g/4oz soup pasta

8-12 large cabbage leaves, washed

1 hard-boiled egg, finely chopped

60g/2oz walnuts, chopped

1 tbsp chopped fresh chives

2 tbsps chopped fresh parsley

1 tsp chopped fresh marjoram

*Salt and freshly ground
black pepper*

280ml/½ pint vegetable stock

1 tbsp walnut oil

1 onion, finely chopped

*1 green pepper,
cored and chopped*

400g/14oz tin chopped tomatoes

*120g/4oz button mushrooms,
chopped*

2 tbsps tomato purée

1 bay leaf

Pinch of sugar

1. Cook the pasta in plenty of lightly salted, boiling water for 8 minutes, or as directed on the packet.

2. Remove the thick stems from the base of the cabbage leaves and then blanch the leaves in boiling water for 3 minutes. Drain and refresh in cold water.

3. When the pasta is cooked, drain well and mix with the egg, walnuts, herbs and seasoning to taste.

4. Divide the pasta mixture between the cabbage leaves, fold up to enclose the filling completely and secure with cocktail sticks.

5. Place in a shallow, ovenproof dish and add the stock. Cover and bake in a preheated 180°C/350°F/Gas mark 4 oven for 40 minutes.

6. Heat the oil in a frying pan, add the onion and pepper and fry for about 5 minutes, until soft. Stir in the remaining ingredients, season and cook gently for 10 minutes.

7. Remove the cabbage parcels from the dish, remove the cocktail sticks and serve with the sauce poured over.

TIME Preparation takes 30 minutes and cooking takes about 1 hour.

Serves 4

Vegetable Stir-fry with Tofu

THE INCLUSION OF TOFU IN THIS RECIPE MAKES IT
AN EXCELLENT PROTEIN MEAL.

Ingredients

60ml/2 fl oz vegetable oil

30g/1oz blanched almonds

1 clove garlic, crushed

120g/4oz baby corn, cut in half

1 red pepper, cored
and sliced

120g/4oz mange tout, trimmed

60g/2oz water chestnuts, sliced

2 heads of broccoli, split
into florets

4 tbsps soy sauce

1 tsp sesame oil

1 tsp sherry

140ml/¼ pint vegetable stock

2 tsps cornflour

120g/4oz bean sprouts

4 spring onions, cut into
thin diagonal slices

225g/8oz tofu, cut into cubes

Salt and freshly ground
black pepper

1. Heat the oil in a wok or frying pan and fry the almonds until browned. Remove with a draining spoon and set aside.

2. Add the garlic and baby corn to the pan, and stir-fry for 1 minute. Stir in the pepper, mange tout, water chestnuts and broccoli florets, and stir-fry for 4 minutes.

3. Mix the soy sauce, sesame oil, sherry, stock and cornflour together in a small dish, and stir until blended. Add to the pan and stir until sauce thickens.

4. Add the bean sprouts, browned almonds, spring onions and tofu, and cook for 3 minutes. Season to taste and serve at once.

TIME Preparation takes about 20 minutes
and cooking takes 10 to 12 minutes.

Asian Ratatouille with Gingered Rice

THIS MEDITERRANEAN-STYLE VEGETABLE STEW IS GIVEN AN ORIENTAL TWIST
WITH SOME WARMING GINGER, SOY SAUCE AND SESAME SEEDS.

Ingredients

75ml/5 tbsps olive oil

1 small red onion, cut into
1.5cm/¾-inch squares

2 garlic cloves, crushed

2.5cm/1-inch piece root ginger,
finely chopped

450g/1lb plum tomatoes, peeled,
seeded and chopped

2 tbsps tamari (Japanese soy
sauce) or dark soy sauce

1½ tbsps rice wine

1 tsp sugar

Salt and freshly ground
black pepper

1 fresh green chilli, seeded and
chopped

2 tsps coriander seeds, crushed

1 small aubergine, cut into
1.5cm/¾-inch chunks

150g/5oz shittake mushrooms, sliced

2 small courgettes, sliced diagonally

1 red pepper, cored and
cut into chunks

2 tsps sesame seeds, toasted

Rice

3 tbsps groundnut oil

1-2 tsps hot chilli oil

2 garlic cloves, crushed

2.5cm/1-inch piece fresh root ginger,
crushed

280g/10oz medium-grain white rice

280ml/½ pint light vegetable stock

280ml/½ pint water

Salt

2 tbsps fresh lime or lemon juice

4 spring onions, finely chopped

2 tbsps finely chopped fresh
coriander leaves

TIME Preparation takes about
35 minutes and cooking takes
45 minutes.

1. Heat 1 tbsp of the olive oil in a saucepan. Add the onion and fry for about 5 minutes, until just soft. Add the garlic and ginger, and fry for 1 minute. Stir in the tomatoes, tamari, rice wine and sugar. Season with salt and pepper. Simmer over a very low heat for 15 to 20 minutes, stirring occasionally, until reduced and thickened.

2. Meanwhile, prepare the rice. Heat the oils in a frying pan with a lid. Add the garlic and root ginger and fry for 1 minute. Add the rice and cook for 3 to 4 minutes, stirring, until all the grains are coated with oil. Pour in the stock, water and a little salt. Bring to the boil, then cover tightly and simmer over very low heat for 15 to 20 minutes, until all the liquid has been absorbed. Remove from the heat and stir in the juice. Leave to stand, covered, for 10 minutes.

3. Meanwhile, heat the remaining olive oil in a large frying pan until very hot. Add the chilli pepper and coriander seeds, and sizzle for 30 seconds. Add the aubergine and shittake mushrooms, and stir-fry over medium heat for 5 minutes. Stir in the remaining vegetables and fry for 3 minutes.

4. When the vegetables are just soft, pour in the tomato sauce, cover and simmer for 10 minutes. Check the seasoning and stir in the sesame seeds.

5. Stir the spring onions and coriander into the rice, and serve with the vegetables.

Serves 4 – 6

Lentil Moussaka

TRY A TASTE OF THE GREEK ISLANDS WITH
THIS VARIATION ON A CLASSIC DISH.

Ingredients

150g/5oz green lentils

1 large aubergine, sliced

4-5 tbsps vegetable oil

1 large onion, chopped

1 clove garlic, crushed

1 large carrot, diced

4 celery sticks, finely chopped

1-2 tsps mixed herbs

400g/14oz tin tomatoes

2 tsps dark soy sauce

Freshly ground black pepper

2 potatoes, cooked and sliced

2 large tomatoes, sliced

Sauce

60g/2oz margarine

4 tbsps brown rice flour

420ml/¾ pint milk

1 large egg, separated

60g/2oz Cheddar cheese, grated

1 tsp nutmeg

1. Cook the lentils in plenty of water until soft. Drain and reserve the liquid.

2. Fry the aubergine in the oil, drain well and set aside. Cook the onion, garlic, carrot and celery in a little of the lentil stock, simmering with the lid on until just tender.

3. Add the lentils, mixed herbs and tinned tomatoes. Simmer gently for 3 to 4 minutes. Season with the soy sauce and pepper.

4. Place a layer of the lentil mixture in a large casserole dish and cover with half the aubergine slices. Cover the aubergine slices with half of the potato slices and all the tomato. Repeat with the remaining lentils, aubergine and potatoes.

5. To make the sauce, gently melt the margarine in a saucepan, remove from the heat and stir in the flour.

6. Return to the heat and add the milk gradually, blending and stirring continuously until the sauce thickens and is lump free. Remove the pan from the heat and cool slightly. Add the egg yolk, stir in the cheese and add the nutmeg.

7. Beat the egg white until it is stiff, then carefully fold into the sauce.

8. Pour the sauce over the moussaka, covering the dish completely. Bake in a preheated 180°C/350°F/Gas mark 4 oven for about 40 minutes, until the top is golden brown.

TIME Preparation takes 45 minutes and cooking takes 1 hour 10 minutes.

Serves 4

Vegetarian Garbure

THIS IS A VEGETARIAN VARIATION OF A CLASSIC FRENCH COUNTRY STEW. SERVED
WITH FRESH WHOLEMEAL BREAD, IT MAKES A WARMING LUNCH OR SUPPER DISH.

Ingredients

225g/8oz haricot beans, soaked
overnight

1 large potato, scrubbed and diced

4 carrots, sliced

2 leeks, washed and chopped

2 tbsps vegetable oil

1 tsp dried marjoram

1 tsp dried thyme

½ tsp paprika pepper

840ml/1½ pints vegetable stock

Salt and freshly ground
black pepper

1 small cabbage, finely shredded

Wholemeal bread, to serve

1. Drain the beans and place them in a
pan with enough fresh water to cover
them by 2.5cm/1 inch. Bring to the
boil, boil rapidly for 10 minutes, then
lower the heat and simmer gently for
1 hour, or until the beans are soft.
Drain and set aside until required.

2. Fry the potato, carrots and leeks in the
oil for 5 minutes. Add the herbs and
paprika, and cook for 1 minute. Stir in
the beans and stock, and simmer gently
for 20 minutes.

3. Stir the bean mixture and season to
taste. Scatter the shredded cabbage over
the beans, cover and continue cooking
for 15 to 20 minutes, until the cabbage
is cooked. Check the seasoning and
serve with the bread.

TIME Preparation takes 20 minutes, plus
overnight soaking. Cooking takes about
1¼ hours.

SERVING IDEA Place thick slices of
bread in the bottom of some soup bowls
and then ladle the Garbure over the
bread – delicious!

Paprika *This brightly coloured spice is made
from capsicums, or red peppers. There are two types of
paprika, hot and sweet, although the type is often not stated on
the label. Hot paprika is obtained by including the inner core and seeds
of the pepper, while sweet paprika is made by adding sugar.*

Serves 4

Parmesan Soufflé Omelette

OMELETTES ARE A WONDERFUL CONVENIENCE FOOD FOR VEGETARIANS. THIS PUFFY
OMELETTE IS FLAVOURED WITH FRESH, CHOPPED CHIVES AND PARMESAN CHEESE.

Ingredients

8 eggs, separated

120ml/4 fl oz milk

90g/3oz grated Parmesan cheese

2 tbsps chopped chives

Salt and freshly ground
black pepper

1 tbsp oil

2 tbsps butter

1. Mix the egg yolks into the milk with the Parmesan, chives, salt and pepper.

2. Whip the egg whites until very stiff and then gently incorporate the yolk mixture into the whites.

3. Heat the oil and the butter in a large frying pan and cook both sides of the omelette until golden brown. Serve immediately.

COOK'S TIP Turning a large omelette like this one can be quite a difficult task. As an alternative, use a small frying pan and cook individual omelettes for your guests, keeping the first ones warm in an open oven.

TIME Preparation takes about 15 minutes and cooking takes 10 to 15 minutes.

Butter *The importance of butter to good cooking cannot be overstressed – without it haute cuisine just would not exist. Butter adds a rich creaminess and distinct flavour to dishes that cannot be matched by margarine, despite what the marketing people may have you believe. The cholesterol content of butter cannot be denied, but, like with all rich foods, moderation is the key.*

Serves 4

Tagliatelle with Blue Cheese Sauce

MANY PASTA DISHES CAN BE RATHER FATTENING. THIS ONE, HOWEVER, USES ONLY
A SMALL AMOUNT OF STRONG CHEESE TO ENHANCE THE PASTA AND SPINACH.

Ingredients

450g/1lb tagliatelle

30g/1oz soft margarine

1 clove garlic, crushed

4 shallots, finely chopped

30g/1oz plain flour

430ml/¾ pint milk

340g/12oz cooked, drained spinach

90g/3oz Stilton cheese, crumbled

*Salt and freshly ground
black pepper*

*Finely chopped fresh parsley,
to garnish*

TIME Preparation takes
15 minutes and cooking takes
15 minutes.

VARIATION Use 1 small
standard or red onion, or a bunch
of spring onions in place of the
shallots.

1. Cook the pasta in a large pan of lightly salted, boiling water for 10 to 12 minutes, until just cooked.

2. Meanwhile, make the spinach and cheese sauce. Melt the margarine in a saucepan, add the garlic and shallots, and cook gently for 5 minutes, stirring.

3. Add the flour and cook for 1 minute, stirring. Remove the pan from the heat and gradually stir in the milk. Heat gently, stirring continuously, until the sauce comes to the boil and thickens. Reduce the heat and simmer gently for 3 minutes, stirring.

4. Press any excess water out of the spinach using the back of a wooden spoon, then chop the spinach. Add the spinach, cheese and seasoning to the sauce and mix well. Reheat gently, stirring continuously, until the cheese has melted and the sauce is piping hot.

5. Drain the cooked pasta thoroughly, toss it with the sauce and serve immediately, garnished with some chopped parsley. Alternatively, serve the pasta with the sauce spooned over it. Serve this dish with crusty bread rolls and a mixed leaf salad.

Serves 4

Spicy Oriental Noodles

THIS VERSATILE CHINESE VEGETABLE DISH MAKES
AN EXCELLENT VEGETARIAN MAIN COURSE.

Ingredients

225g/8oz Chinese noodles
(medium thickness)

75ml/5 tbsps oil

4 carrots, cut into thinly sliced
rounds

225g/8oz broccoli, cut into florets

4 spring onions, diagonally sliced

12 Chinese mushrooms,
soaked 30 minutes

1 clove garlic, peeled

1-2 tsps chilli sauce, mild or hot

4 tbsps soy sauce

4 tbsps rice wine or dry sherry

2 tsps cornflour

1. Cook the noodles in boiling, salted water for about 4 to 5 minutes. Drain well, rinse under hot water to remove starch and drain again. Toss with about 1 tbsp of the oil to prevent sticking.

2. Place the carrots, broccoli and spring onions in boiling water for about 2 minutes to blanch. Drain and rinse under cold water to stop them cooking, and leave to drain dry. Remove and discard the mushroom stems and slice the caps thinly. Set aside with the other vegetables.

3. Heat a wok and add the remaining oil with the garlic clove. Leave the garlic in the pan while the oil heats and them remove it. Add the carrots and broccoli, and stir-fry about 1 minute. Add mushrooms and onions, and continue to stir-fry, tossing the vegetables in the pan continuously.

4. Combine the chilli sauce, soy sauce, wine and cornflour, mixing well. Pour over the vegetables and cook until the sauce clears. Add the noodles, toss together well to heat them through and serve immediately.

Time Preparation takes about 25 minutes
and cooking takes 7 to 8 minutes.

Noodles *A mainstay of the Chinese diet, noodles are available in various forms, with the quick-cooking egg-thread noodles and rice noodles being particularly popular. Many types of noodle are sold in compressed blocks, having been pre-steamed before packing.*

Serves 4

Vegetable Chop Suey

WITH VEGETABLES, SIMPLE TREATMENTS ARE USUALLY THE BEST. HERE, STIR-FRIED VEGETABLES ARE SIMMERED IN A WOK WITH STOCK AND SOY SAUCE.

Ingredients

2 tbsps vegetable oil

1 green pepper, cored and thinly sliced

1 red pepper, cored and thinly sliced

2 cloves garlic, finely chopped

1 onion, thinly sliced

1 carrot, thinly sliced

½ cucumber, thinly sliced

1 courgette, central core discarded and flesh thinly sliced

2 tsps sugar

2 tbsps soy sauce

120ml/4 fl oz vegetable stock

Salt and freshly ground black pepper

1. Heat the oil in a wok and stir-fry the peppers and garlic for 30 seconds. Add the onion and carrot, and stir-fry for another 30 seconds.

2. Add the cucumber and the courgette, and cook for 1 minute, stirring and shaking the wok continuously.

3. Stir in the sugar, soy sauce, vegetable stock, salt and pepper, mixing together well. Simmer until all the ingredients are heated through. Serve piping hot.

COOK'S TIP If you follow the order given above for cooking the vegetables, they will be cooked but still slightly crisp.

TIME Preparation takes about 15 minutes and cooking takes 5 minutes.

Cinnamon *This useful spice is obtained from the bark of the cinnamon tree (cinnamon sticks are rolled pieces of bark), which grows wild in Sri Lanka and southern India. It has been valued for its subtle flavour for centuries and was at one point among the most valuable commodities traded between Sri Lanka and Europe.*

Serves 4

Saagwalla Daal

SPINACH AND DAAL COMPLEMENT EACH OTHER WELL. THE DISH IS EASY TO MAKE AND
FULL OF ESSENTIAL NUTRIENTS. IF MOONG DAAL IS UNAVAILABLE, USE YELLOW SPLIT PEAS.

Ingredients

180g/6oz skinless split moong daal
or yellow split peas

2 heaped tbsps ghee or
unsalted butter

1 large onion, finely sliced

1 fresh green chilli, sliced lengthways

2 cinnamon sticks, broken up
into 2-3 pieces

½ tsp ground turmeric

½ tsp garam masala

¼ tsp chilli powder

1 tsp salt or to taste

1 tsp ground cumin

2 ripe tomatoes, peeled and chopped

570ml/1 pint warm water

2 tbsps cooking oil

½ tsp mustard seeds

2-3 cloves garlic, finely chopped

1-2 dried red chillies,
coarsely chopped

150g/5oz leaf spinach, defrosted
and finely chopped, or 280g/10oz
fresh spinach, stalks removed
and finely chopped

1. Wash the daal, soak it for 1½ to
   2 hours and then drain well.

2. Melt the ghee or butter in a nonstick or
   cast iron frying pan, add the onions,
   chilli and cinnamon, and fry for 6 to 8
   minutes until the onions are lightly
   browned.

3. Add the turmeric and garam masala, stir
   and mix well. Add the daal, chilli
   powder and salt. Stir and fry for
   8 to 10 minutes over low heat.

4. Add the cumin and tomato, stir and
   cook for 3 to 4 minutes.

5. Add the water, bring to the boil, cover
   and simmer for 30 to 35 minutes,
   stirring occasionally.

6. Meanwhile, heat the oil over medium
   heat and fry the mustard seeds until
   they pop. Add the garlic and allow it to
   turn slightly brown.

7. Add the dried chillies and spinach, and
   stir and mix thoroughly. Cover the pan
   and simmer for 5 minutes.

8. Add the spinach to the daal, cover and
   cook over low heat for 10 minutes,
   stirring occasionally. Remove the pan
   from heat and serve.

TIME Preparation takes 10 to 15 minutes,
plus time needed to soak the daal.
Cooking takes 1 hour 10 minutes.

Serves 2

Vegetable Enchiladas

TEX-MEX COOKING INCLUDES SOME WONDERFUL SAUCES.
HERE, A REFRESHING SALSA COMPLEMENTS A VEGETABLE FILLING.

Ingredients

4 tortillas

Soured cream to serve

Green chilli salsa

1 tbsp oil

3 tomatillos (or unripe tomatoes), husks removed and sliced

1 clove garlic

30g/1oz ground coriander

2 green chillies, cored

Juice of 1 lime

120ml/4 fl oz soured cream

Pinch of salt and sugar

Filling

2 tbsps vegetable oil

1 small onion, finely chopped

1 green pepper, cored and diced

2 courgettes, diced

½ tsp oregano

½ tsp ground cumin

120g/4oz sweetcorn

Salt and freshly ground
black pepper

180g/6oz mild cheese, grated

1. Heat the oil for the salsa in a small frying pan and sauté the tomatillos for about 3 minutes to soften. Place in a food processor or blender with the garlic, coriander, chillies and lime juice. Purée until smooth. Fold in the soured cream, add seasoning and chill.

2. Wrap the tortillas in foil and re-heat in a moderate oven for about 10 minutes.

3. For the filling, heat the oil, add the onion and cook to soften. Add the remaining vegetables, except the sweetcorn. Add the oregano and cumin, and cook about 3 minutes, or until the onions are soft. Add the sweetcorn and heat through. Season to taste and stir in the cheese.

4. Fill the tortillas with the mixture and place in a baking dish. Cook, covered, in a preheated 180°C/350°F/Gas mark 4 oven for about 10 to 15 minutes, until the cheese has melted and the filling bubbles.

5. Remove the enchiladas from the oven and serve topped with soured cream and the green chilli salsa.

TIME Preparation takes about 20 minutes and cooking takes about 30 minutes.

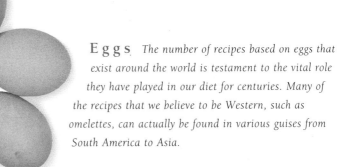

Eggs *The number of recipes based on eggs that exist around the world is testament to the vital role they have played in our diet for centuries. Many of the recipes that we believe to be Western, such as omelettes, can actually be found in various guises from South America to Asia.*

Serves 6

Cheese Soufflé

THIS PUFFY, GOLDEN SOUFFLÉ WILL DELIGHT YOUR GUESTS, BUT RUSH
IT TO THE TABLE IMMEDIATELY ON REMOVAL FROM THE OVEN!

Ingredients

Butter for greasing

180g/6oz cheese, grated

30g/1oz butter

1 tbsp plain flour

280ml/½ pint milk

Salt and freshly ground
black pepper

Pinch of nutmeg

4 eggs, separated

1 extra egg white

1. Grease a soufflé dish with butter and
sprinkle with 3 tbsps of the grated
cheese.

2. Melt the butter in a heavy saucepan,
mix in the flour, cook for about
1 minute, pour in all the milk and beat
continuously until the mixture
thickens. Reduce the heat and cook
for 2 minutes.

3. Add the salt, pepper and nutmeg. Add
the egg yolks one by one, beating well
with a wooden spoon. Leave to cool for
about 5 minutes.

4. Stir the remaining cheese into the white
sauce. Whisk the 5 egg whites until
firm, then fold them gently into the
cheese mixture with a metal spoon.

5. Pour the mixture into the prepared
soufflé dish and cook in a preheated
190°C/375°F/Gas mark 5 oven for
40 to 45 minutes. The soufflé should
be well risen and golden on top. Serve
immediately.

SERVING IDEA At step 5, the mixture
could be poured into 6 individual
buttered and 'cheesed' ramekins. Cooking
time will be reduced to 20 to
25 minutes.

TIME Preparation takes about 20 minutes,
and cooking takes 40 to 45 minutes.

Serves 6

Black Bean and Squash Casserole

EAST MEETS WEST IN THIS UNUSUAL DISH, WHICH MIXES AROMATIC SPICES WITH
FAMILIAR ROOT VEGETABLES.

Ingredients

280g/10oz cooked black
turtle beans

1 tsp cumin seeds

2 tsps coriander seeds

1 tbsp sesame seeds

2 tsps dried oregano

2 tbsps olive oil

1 onion, chopped

2 garlic cloves, crushed

1-2 fresh red chillies,
seeded and chopped

1 butternut squash or small
pumpkin, weighing about
550g/1¼lbs, peeled and
cut into chunks

1 yellow yam or sweet potato,
peeled and cut into chunks

2 large carrots, thickly sliced

2 potatoes, peeled and
cut into chunks

1 celeriac, weighing
about 450g/1lb, peeled and
cut into chunks

90g/3oz frozen sweetcorn

400g/14oz tin chopped tomatoes

340ml/12 fl oz vegetable stock

Salt and freshly ground
black pepper

4 tbsps chopped fresh
coriander leaves

2 tbsps lime juice

1. Heat the seeds in a small frying pan for 1 to 2 minutes. Add the oregano and heat for a few more seconds. Remove and crush.

2. Heat the oil in a casserole, add the onion and fry until translucent. Add the garlic and chillies, and fry for 2 to 3 minutes.

3. Add the seeds and remaining ingredients, except the coriander leaves and lime juice. Bring to the boil, cover and simmer for 45 minutes. Add the coriander and lime juice just before serving.

TIME Preparation takes 25 minutes. Cooking takes 1 hour 20 minutes.

Squash More and more varieties of squash are now finding their way into our supermarkets. Squashes, however, no matter how colourful or exotic in shape, are almost always somewhat bland in flavour and benefit from robust treatment.

Serves 4

Red Bean Creole

CREOLE COOKING IS A BLEND OF AFRICAN, CARIBBEAN AND INDIAN CUISINE THAT REFLECTS PAST TRADING LINKS. THE EMPHASIS IS ON SPICING UP LOCAL INGREDIENTS.

Ingredients

180g/6oz long-grain brown or white rice

30g/1oz butter or margarine

1 green pepper, cored and sliced

120g/4oz mushrooms, sliced

Pinch of cayenne pepper

Pinch of ground nutmeg

340g/12oz cooked red kidney beans

140ml/¼ pint vegetable stock

4 firm tomatoes, peeled, seeded and cut into strips

4 spring onions, trimmed and chopped

Salt and freshly ground black pepper

Chopped fresh parsley to garnish

1. Cook the rice in plenty of boiling water as directed on the packet. Drain and rinse with boiling water.

2. Melt the butter in a large saucepan, add the pepper and mushrooms, and cook for about 5 minutes, until just beginning to soften.

3. Add the rice, cayenne pepper, nutmeg, beans and stock. Cook gently for 10 minutes, stir in the remaining ingredients and cook for another 5 minutes to heat all the ingredients thoroughly. Serve garnished with chopped parsley.

SERVING IDEA Serve with a small side salad or a bowl of ratatouille.

TIME Preparation takes 20 minutes and cooking takes about 40 minutes.

Nutmeg *Nutmeg is obtained from the seed of a tree cultivated in tropical regions. The fruits are harvested when ripe, the outer shell is removed and the seeds allowed to dry. Nutmeg has a strong aroma and is used only in small quantities.*

Serves 4

Gado Gado

THIS DELICIOUS INDONESIAN DISH HAS BECOME A FIRM VEGETARIAN FAVOURITE.
IT IS HEALTHY, EASY TO PREPARE AND A REAL TASTE BUD TICKLER.

Ingredients

2 tbsps peanut oil

2 carrots, cut into thin strips

2 potatoes, cut into thin strips

225g/8oz green beans, trimmed

225g/8oz Chinese leaves, shredded

225g/8oz bean sprouts

Half a cucumber, cut into batons

Peanut sauce

60ml/2 fl oz peanut oil

120g/4oz raw shelled peanuts

4 red chillies, seeded and
finely chopped

4 shallots, finely chopped

2 cloves garlic, crushed

140ml/¼ pint water

2 tsps brown sugar

Juice of half a lemon

Salt

225ml/8 fl oz coconut milk

Garnish

Sliced hard-boiled eggs

Sliced cucumbers

1. Heat a wok and add 2 tbsps peanut oil. When hot, add the carrot and potato. Stir-fry for 2 minutes, then add green beans and Chinese leaves. Cook for 3 minutes.

2. Add the bean sprouts and cucumber, and stir-fry for 2 minutes. Remove the vegetables, place in a serving dish and chill.

3. Re-heat the wok, add the remaining peanut oil, and fry the peanuts for 2 to 3 minutes. Remove and drain on kitchen paper. Blend or pound the chillies, shallots and garlic to a smooth paste. Grind or blend the peanuts to a powder.

4. Re-heat the peanut oil, add the chilli paste and fry for 2 minutes. Add the water and bring to the boil. Add the peanuts, brown sugar, lemon juice and salt to taste. Heat, stirring until sauce is thick – about 10 minutes – and add the coconut milk.

5. Garnish the vegetables with slices of hard-boiled egg and cucumber, and serve with the peanut sauce.

TIME Preparation takes 20 minutes and cooking takes 30 minutes.

Serves 2 – 3

Cauliflower Masala

CAULIFLOWER IS PARTICULARLY DELICIOUS CURRIED, WHEN IT SEEMS TO SOAK UP
ALL THE FLAVOURS WHILE RETAINING ITS CHARACTERISTIC TEXTURE.

Ingredients

60ml/2 fl oz vegetable oil

1 tsp cumin seeds

1 large onion, chopped

½ tsp ground turmeric

1 tsp ground coriander

1 tsp ground cumin

¼-½ tsp chilli powder

2 ripe tomatoes, peeled
and chopped

2 potatoes, peeled and cut into
thick batons

180ml/6 fl oz warm water

1 cauliflower, cut into florets

120g/4oz peas, fresh or
frozen (cook fresh peas until
they are tender before using)

1-2 fresh green chillies, seeded
and split lengthways into halves

1 tsp salt or to taste

½ tsp garam masala

1 tbsp chopped fresh coriander
leaves

1. Heat the oil over medium heat and add the cumin seeds. As soon as they start popping, add the onion and fry for about 5 minutes until soft.

2. Turn heat down to low and add the turmeric, coriander, cumin and chilli powder. Stir and fry for 2 to 3 minutes and add the chopped tomatoes. Fry for another 2 to 3 minutes, stirring continuously.

3. Add the potatoes and the water. Bring to the boil, cover the pan and simmer until the potatoes are half cooked.

4. Add the cauliflower, cover the pan again and simmer for about 10 minutes, until the potatoes are tender.

5. Stir in the peas, chillies, salt and garam masala. Cover and cook for 5 minutes. Remove from the heat and stir in the chopped coriander.

TIME Preparation takes about 25 minutes and cooking takes 30 to 35 minutes.

VARIATION Cook in 3 tbsps ghee or unsalted butter instead of oil for a richer flavour.

Serves 4–6

Egg and Potato Dum

HARD-BOILED, CURRIED EGGS ARE VERY POPULAR IN NORTHEAST INDIA,
WHERE THIS RECIPE ORIGINATES.

Ingredients

6 hard-boiled eggs

75ml/5 tbsps cooking oil

3 potatoes, peeled and quartered

⅛ tsp each of chilli powder and
ground turmeric, mixed together

1 large onion, finely chopped

2.5cm/½-inch cube root ginger,
peeled and grated

1 cinnamon stick, broken up into
2-3 pieces

2 black or green cardamoms,
split open at the top

4 whole cloves

1 fresh green chilli, chopped

1 small tin tomatoes

½ tsp ground turmeric

2 tsps ground coriander

1 tsp ground fennel

¼-½ tsp chilli powder (optional)

1 tsp salt or to taste

225ml/8 fl oz warm water

1 tbsp chopped fresh coriander
leaves

1. Shell the eggs and make 4 slits lengthways on each egg, leaving about 1cm/½-inch gap at either end.

2. Heat the oil over medium heat in a cast-iron or nonstick frying pan. Fry the potatoes until they are well browned on all sides, about 10 minutes. Remove with a slotted spoon and set aside.

3. Remove pan from the heat and stir in the turmeric and chilli mixture. Place the pan on the heat and fry the whole eggs until they are well browned. Remove with a slotted spoon and set aside.

4. In the same oil, fry the onions, ginger, cinnamon, cardamom, cloves and green chilli for 6 to 7 minutes, until the onions are lightly browned.

5. Add half the tomatoes, stir and fry until the tomatoes break up. Add the turmeric, ground coriander, fennel and chilli powder. Stir and fry for 3 to 4 minutes. Add the remaining tomatoes and fry for 4 to 5 minutes, stirring frequently.

6. Add the potatoes, salt and water, bring to the boil, cover the pan tightly and simmer until the potatoes are tender, stirring occasionally.

7. Add the eggs and simmer, uncovered, for 5 to 6 minutes, stirring once or twice. Stir in the coriander leaves and serve.

TIME Preparation takes 15 minutes and cooking takes 35 to 40 minutes.

Eastern Mediterranean Casserole

BURSTING WITH COLOUR AND FLAVOUR, THIS COMFORTING CASSEROLE
MAKES AN EXCELLENT ENTRÉE FOR AN AUTUMN DINNER.

Ingredients

1 tsp cumin seeds

2 tsps coriander seeds

1 tbsp sesame seeds

2 tsps dried oregano

1 tsp vegetable oil

1 onion, chopped

3 garlic cloves, finely chopped

1 green chilli, seeded and chopped

340ml/12 fl oz strong vegetable stock

225g/8oz butternut squash or pumpkin flesh, cut into chunks

1 small aubergine, cut into chunks

1 red pepper, cut into squares

180g/6oz green beans, chopped

180g/6oz small new potatoes

400g/14oz tin chopped tomatoes

Salt and freshly ground black pepper

180g/6oz shredded green cabbage

1. Place the seeds in a small, heavy-based pan without any oil. Heat until the aroma rises. Add the oregano and dry-fry for a few more seconds. Remove from the heat, crush with a pestle and mortar, and set aside.

2. Heat the oil in a heavy-based, nonstick casserole. Gently fry the onion for a few minutes over medium-low heat until translucent. Add the garlic, chilli and 2 tbsp of the stock. Fry for 3 minutes, or until soft. Stir in the seed mixture.

3. Add the squash, aubergine, pepper, beans, potatoes and tomatoes. Bring to the boil, cover and cook over medium-low heat for 10 minutes.

4. Pour in the remaining stock and season with salt and pepper. Bring to the boil, then cover and simmer for 20 minutes.

Add more stock if the mixture starts to look too dry.

5. Stir in the cabbage and cook for 2 to 3 minutes, until just wilted but still bright green. Serve immediately with cooked rice or cracked wheat.

TIME Preparation takes 25 minutes and cooking takes 45 minutes.

VARIATION Use 225g/8oz chopped mushrooms in place of the aubergine.

COOK'S TIP The toasted crushed seeds act as a thickener and also add a wonderfully earthy flavour to the dish.

Serves 4

Japanese Steamer

THE JAPANESE ARE RENOWNED FOR THEIR ELEGANT CUISINE, AND THIS SIMPLE
RECIPE IS NO EXCEPTION. SERVE FOR A DELICIOUS ORIENTAL-STYLE MEAL.

Ingredients

120g/4oz buckwheat noodles

16 dried shittake mushrooms,
soaked overnight

120g/4oz button mushrooms

8 baby corn, halved lengthways

1 small daikon (mooli) radish,
sliced

340g/12oz tofu, drained

1 packet dried sea spinach,
soaked for 1 hour

140ml/¼ pint Japanese soy sauce

Small piece fresh root ginger,
peeled and grated

60ml/2 fl oz vegetable stock

1 tbsp sherry

1 tsp cornflour

1 lemon, thinly sliced

1 small bunch fresh chives

1. Cook the noodles in plenty of lightly salted, boiling water for 10 minutes.

2. Remove the stems from the shittake mushrooms and discard. Steam the mushroom caps, button mushrooms, baby corn and daikon for 5 to 10 minutes.

3. Cut the tofu into chunks and steam with the sea spinach for 2 minutes.

4. Make the sauce by heating the soy sauce, root ginger and vegetable stock in a small pan until simmering. Blend the sherry and cornflour together, add to the pan and cook until thickened.

5. Drain the noodles and arrange along with the steamed vegetables on serving plates. Pour a little sauce over each and serve remaining sauce separately. Garnish with lemon slices and chives.

TIME Preparation takes about 30 minutes, plus overnight soaking. Cooking takes about 15 minutes.

Chives Chives are related to the onion and leek but impart a more subtle flavour. As well as the standard variety of chive sold in supermarkets, you may also come across a dark green variety known as Chinese or garlic chives. This is a larger plant whose flattish leaves have a pronounced garlic flavour.

Serves 6

Aubergine Bake

IT MAY SEEM A CRIME TO ALL THOSE WHO LOVE THE FLAVOUR OF AUBERGINE, BUT THIS WONDERFUL VEGETABLE WAS ONCE TREATED SIMPLY AS A DECORATIVE PLANT!

Ingredients

2 large or 3 medium aubergines

2½ tsps salt

140ml/¼ pint malt vinegar

2 tbsps vegetable oil

2 large onions, sliced into rings

2 green chillies, seeded and finely chopped

400g/14oz tin peeled plum tomatoes, chopped

¾ tsp chilli powder

2 tsps crushed garlic

¾ tsp ground turmeric

8 tomatoes, sliced

280ml/½ pint natural yogurt

1¼ tsps freshly ground black pepper

90g/3oz Cheddar cheese, finely grated

1. Cut the aubergines into 0.5cm/¼-inch-thick slices. Arrange the slices in a shallow dish and sprinkle with 1½ tsps of the salt. Pour over the malt vinegar, cover the dish, and marinate for 30 minutes. Drain the aubergine well, discarding the marinade.

2. Heat the oil in a frying pan and gently fry the onion rings until golden brown. Add the chillies, remaining salt, chopped tomatoes, chilli powder, garlic and turmeric. Mix well and simmer for 5 to 7 minutes until thick and well blended.

3. Remove the sauce from the heat and cool slightly. Blend to a smooth purée using a food processor or blender.

4. Arrange half of the aubergine slices in the base of a greased shallow ovenproof dish. Spoon half of the tomato sauce over the aubergine slices. Cover this with the remaining aubergine, then top with the remaining tomato sauce and sliced tomatoes.

5. Mix together the yogurt, black pepper and cheese, and pour over the tomato slices.

6. Bake in a preheated 190°C/375°F/Gas mark 5 oven for 20 to 30 minutes, until the cheese topping bubbles and turns golden brown. Serve hot, straight from the oven.

TIME Preparation takes about 30 minutes and cooking takes 40 minutes.

PREPARATION Make sure that the aubergines are well drained of excess vinegar by pressing them into a colander using the back of your hand. Do not rinse them, however, as the vinegar gives a tangy flavour to the dish.

Serves 4

Mushroom Stroganoff

WITH MUSHROOMS REPLACING THE MEAT, THIS DELICIOUS STROGANOFF IS TASTIER
AND HEALTHIER THAN THE ORIGINAL RECIPE.

Ingredients

60g/2oz butter or margarine

2 onions, sliced

5 celery sticks, chopped

450g/1lb button mushrooms

½ tsp dried mixed herbs

½ tsp dried basil

1 heaped tbsp plain flour

280ml/½ pint stock

Salt and freshly ground
black pepper

65ml/2½ fl oz soured cream or
natural yogurt

Chopped fresh parsley,
to garnish

TIME Preparation takes 10 minutes and
cooking takes 20 minutes.

1. Melt the butter or margarine in a large
   pan, add the onions and celery,
   and sauté over a low heat until the
   onions are transparent.

2. Add the mushrooms and cook for 2 to
   3 minutes, until the juices run. Add the
   mixed herbs and basil, stir in the flour,
   and heat for 1 minute.

3. Add the stock and seasoning, and cook
   gently for 8 to 10 minutes. Remove from
   the heat, stir in the soured cream, and
   adjust the seasoning if necessary.

4. Heat very gently to serving temperature,
   but do not allow to boil. Garnish with the
   chopped parsley and serve at once.

Celery *It is thought celery was first widely eaten
during the Middle Ages, when it began to be cultivated.
It is rich in mineral salts, vitamins and iron and, although
often served raw, it is not easily digestible in this
form and is better cooked.*

SIDE DISHES

Side dishes are all too often overlooked by busy cooks, yet they undoubtedly add an extra dimension to a meal, both in terms of nutrition and taste. Most people enjoy dipping into a variety of different dishes, and serving vegetables, breads and rice with a contrasting main course produces a much more interesting meal. In this chapter you will find a cross-section of side dishes from around the world, including an Indian Carrot Pilau, Roasted Vegetables from the Mediterranean, and delicious Long Beans in Coconut Milk from Thailand. Also included are a number of easy-to-prepare breads from as far afield as Ireland, India and Mexico.

Serves 6

Baked Pineapple Rice

THIS ATTRACTIVELY PRESENTED RICE DISH IS FROM
BANGKOK AND THE CENTRAL PLAINS OF THAILAND.

Ingredients

1 pineapple

2 tbsps oil

1 clove garlic, crushed

4 shallots, chopped

450g/1lb cooked rice

140ml/¼ pint thick coconut milk

60g/2oz raisins

60g/2oz toasted cashew nuts

Yellow curry paste

2 tbsps cumin seeds

2 tbsps coriander seeds

3 stems lemon grass, chopped

1 tbsp grated fresh root ginger

6 red chillies, seeded
and chopped

1 tsp salt

3 cloves garlic, crushed

1 small shallot, finely chopped

1 tsp ground turmeric

1. Dry-fry the cumin and coriander seeds for 3 to 4 minutes, shaking the pan to prevent them burning. Remove from the heat and set aside. Place the lemon grass and ginger in a pestle and mortar, and pound together well. Add the chillies and salt, and pound again. Add the chillies, shallot, ground spices and turmeric, and pound all together well. Set aside.

2. Cut the pineapple in half lengthways, keeping the leaves attached. Scoop out the flesh using a tablespoon and a paring knife to leave two shells with a thin border of flesh attached. Chop half the flesh to use later in the dish (the remainder is not needed for this recipe).

3. Heat the oil in a wok and fry the garlic and shallots until softened. Stir in 1 tbsp of curry paste and fry for 1 minute. Add the rice and toss together with the shallot mixture. Stir in the coconut milk, raisins, chopped pineapple and cashew nuts.

4. Pile the mixture into the pineapple shells. Wrap the pineapple leaves in foil to stop them burning and place on a baking sheet. Bake in a preheated 160°C/325°F/Gas mark 3 oven for 20 minutes.

TIME Preparation takes 20 minutes and cooking takes about 25 minutes.

Makes 1 Small Loaf

Irish Soda Bread

TRADITIONALLY THE IRISH ARE DAILY BAKERS
AND THIS IS THEIR EVERYDAY BREAD.

Ingredients

225g/8oz plain flour

½ tsp salt

1 tsp bicarbonate of soda

½ tsp cream of tartar

1 tbsp butter

180ml/6 fl oz buttermilk

1. Mix the flour, salt, bicarbonate of soda and cream of tartar together in a bowl, then rub in the butter. Pour in the buttermilk and mix to a soft dough with a metal spatula. Turn out onto a floured surface and shape into a round – do not knead the dough. Place on a floured baking sheet and score a cross in the top of the loaf using a sharp knife. Sprinkle lightly with flour.

2. Bake in a preheated 220°C/425°F/Gas mark 7 oven oven for 10 minutes. Turn the oven down to 200°C/400°F/Gas mark 6 and bake for another 10 minutes. Cool on a wire rack.

TIME Preparation takes 10 to 15 minutes and cooking takes about 20 minutes.

COOK'S TIP To make a light soda bread, it is important to mix it as quickly and lightly as possible.

Serves 6

Sri Lankan Rice

SERVE THIS RICE DISH HOT AS AN ACCOMPANIMENT
TO VEGETABLE CURRIES OR PULSE DISHES.

Ingredients

2 tbsps sunflower oil

1 small onion, finely chopped

1 clove garlic, crushed

½ tsp ground cumin

½ tsp ground coriander

½ tsp paprika

1 tsp turmeric

Large pinch of chilli or
cayenne pepper

90g/3oz basmati rice, washed
and drained

180ml/6 fl oz skimmed milk

½ tsp salt

Freshly ground black pepper
to taste

120g/4oz mange tout, trimmed
and cut in half

90g/3oz button mushrooms, sliced

60g/2oz sweetcorn

30g/1oz raisins, washed
and soaked

1. Heat the oil in a large nonstick
   saucepan. Add the onion and garlic
   and fry gently for 4 to 5 minutes.

2. Add the cumin, coriander, paprika,
   turmeric and chilli, and fry for another
   3 to 4 minutes – do not allow the
   mixture to burn.

3. Add the washed rice and mix well
   with the onions and spices for about
   2 minutes.

4. Add the milk and salt and pepper, stir
   gently and bring to the boil. Cover the
   pan and simmer until all the liquid is
   absorbed and the rice is cooked,
   approximately 15 to 20 minutes.

5. While the rice is cooking, steam the
   mange tout, mushrooms, corn and
   raisins. Add the vegetables to the rice
   and gently mix through.

6. Serve immediately or transfer to a
   serving dish to cool.

TIME Preparation takes 15 minutes and
cooking takes about 25 minutes.

Right: Sri Lankan Rice

Serves 6

Refried Beans

BEANS ARE ONE OF MEXICO'S MOST IMPORTANT
INGREDIENTS, AND REFRIED BEANS IS A CLASSIC
ACCOMPANIMENT TO NUMEROUS MEXICAN AND
TEX-MEX MAIN COURSES.

Ingredients

225g/8oz dried pinto beans

Water to cover

1 bay leaf

90ml/3 fl oz oil

Salt and freshly ground
black pepper

Grated mild cheese

Shredded lettuce

Tortillas

TIME Preparation takes about
15 minutes. The beans must be
soaked overnight or rehydrated by
the quick method. They must be
cooked at least 2 hours before
frying.

1. Soak the beans overnight. Change the
water, add the bay leaf and bring to the
boil. Cover and simmer about 2 hours,
or until the beans are completely
tender. Alternatively, bring the beans to
the boil in cold water and then allow to
boil rapidly for 10 minutes. Cover and
leave to stand for 1 hour. Change the
water and then continue with the
recipe. Drain the beans and reserve a
small amount of the cooking liquid.
Discard the bay leaf.

2. Heat the oil in a heavy frying pan. Add
the beans and, as they fry, mash them
with the back of a spoon. Do not over-
mash; about a third of the beans should
stay whole. Season to taste.

3. Smooth out the beans in the pan and
cook until the bottom is set but not
browned. Turn the beans over and cook
the other side.

4. Top with the cheese and cook the
beans until the cheese melts.

Serves 4

Roasted Vegetables

THE FLAVOURS AND COLOURS OF CRISP MEDITERRANEAN-STYLE VEGETABLES
ARE COMBINED IN THIS DELICIOUS AND NUTRITIOUS RECIPE.

Ingredients

1 red onion, sliced

1 white or yellow onion, sliced

4 courgettes, thickly sliced

225g/8oz baby corn

1 aubergine, cut into chunks

1 red pepper, cored and
cut into large dice

1 yellow pepper, cored
and cut into large dice

2 cloves garlic, thinly sliced

4 tsps olive oil

Salt and freshly ground
black pepper

2-3 tbsps chopped, mixed
fresh herbs

TIME Preparation takes
10 minutes and cooking takes
20 to 30 minutes.

1. Place all the vegetables and garlic in a
nonstick roasting pan and mix together.

2. Add the oil and seasoning and toss to
lightly coat the vegetables with oil.

3. Bake in a preheated oven at 220°C/
425°F/Gas mark 7 for 20 to 30 minutes,

until just tender and tinged brown at
the edges. Stir once or twice during
cooking.

4. Sprinkle with the herbs and toss to
mix. Serve hot or cold.

Serves 6

Noodles with Poppy Seeds and Raisins

THIS TRADITIONAL POLISH DISH MAKES AN UNUSUAL BUT DELICIOUS
ACCOMPANIMENT, OR IT COULD BE SERVED AS A SNACK.

Ingredients

225g/8oz noodles or
other pasta shapes

Pinch of salt

1 tbsp oil

140ml/¼ pint double cream

90g/3oz black poppy seeds,
ground

2 tbsps honey

90g/3oz raisins

1. Bring lots of water to the boil in a large saucepan with a pinch of salt. Add the oil and the noodles or other pasta shapes, and bring back to the boil. Cook, uncovered, for about 10 to 12 minutes until tender.

2. Drain the pasta and rinse under hot water. If using immediately, allow to drain dry. If not, place in a bowl of water to keep.

3. Place the double cream in a deep, heavy-based saucepan and bring almost to the boil.

4. When the cream reaches scalding point, mix in the poppy seeds, honey and raisins. Cook slowly for about 5 minutes, or until the mixture becomes thick but will still fall off a spoon easily.

5. Toss the poppy seed mixture with the noodles and serve hot.

TIME Preparation takes about 15 minutes
and cooking takes about 15 minutes.

Makes One Loaf

Roman Focaccia

THIS CLASSIC ITALIAN BREAD IS TOPPED WITH THINLY SLICED
RAW ONION THAT BAKES TO A GOLDEN BROWN IN THE OVEN.

Ingredients

30g/1oz fresh yeast

225ml/ 8 fl oz warm water

450g/1lb strong plain flour

1 tsp salt

75ml/5 tbsps fruity olive oil

2 large onions, very thinly sliced

1 large sprig fresh rosemary

Coarse sea salt

1. Crumble the yeast into the warm water, leave for 3 to 4 minutes, then stir to completely dissolve the yeast.

2. Mix the flour and salt together and make a well in the centre. Add 60ml/ 4 tbsps of the olive oil and the yeast liquid, and mix together into a manageable dough.

3. Turn out onto a lightly floured surface and knead until smooth and elastic. Return the dough to the bowl, cover and leave in a warm place until doubled in bulk – about 1 hour.

4. Place the onion slices in cold water and soak for at least 30 minutes.

5. Knock the dough back and roll it out to fit an oiled baking pan about 40 x 25cm/ 16 x 10 inches. Lift the dough into the pan, pressing it well into the corners. Cover and leave in a warm place to rise for 20 to 30 minutes. Drain the onion slices and dry them.

6. Brush the dough with the remaining oil and top with the onion slices. Strip the rosemary leaves from the stalk and chop finely. Scatter them over the onions with some coarse sea salt.

7. Bake in a preheated 220°C/425°F/Gas mark 7 oven for 20 to 30 minutes, until the onions are soft and the bread is a pale golden brown. Cool on a wire rack.

VARIATION Sprinkle 30g/1oz freshly grated Parmesan over the onion topping before baking.

TIME Preparation takes about 2¼ hours and cooking takes 20 to 30 minutes.

Makes 18 Small Breads

Pita Bread

THESE ARE THE BEST KNOWN OF ALL THE FLAT BREADS. THEY ARE EATEN
THROUGHOUT THE MEDITERRANEAN WITH DIPS AND BARBECUED MEATS.

Ingredients

15g/½oz fresh yeast

280ml/½ pint warm water

450g/1lb flour

½ tsp salt

1. Crumble the yeast into half the water and stir until completely dissolved. Leave in a warm place, loosely covered, until the yeast bubbles – about 20 minutes.

2. Mix the flour and salt in a bowl, and gradually add the yeast mixture. Stir with a wooden spoon, while adding the rest of the water to form a stiff dough.

3. Knead the dough until it is smooth and elastic. Divide the dough into 18 pieces, cover and leave in a warm place for 30 minutes.

4. Roll out each piece of dough on a floured board to form a thin round. Sprinkle lightly with more flour, cover and leave for 1 hour.

5. Flatten the rounds and roll out again, then cover and leave for another 30 minutes.

6. Bake the pita breads in batches on a floured baking sheet at the top of a preheated 250°C/500°F/Gas mark 9 oven for about 10 minutes; they will puff up but will flatten immediately when removed from the oven.

TIME Preparation takes about 3 hours and cooking takes 10 minutes per batch.

COOK'S TIP Do not allow the pitas to brown too much during baking – they should be only slightly browned.

VARIATION Use the dough to make just 12 breads if you prefer your pitas slightly thicker.

Makes 8

Naan Bread

THESE BREADS FROM INDIA ARE TRADITIONALLY COOKED IN A CLAY OVEN CALLED A
TANDOOR, BUT A VERY HOT CONVENTIONAL OVEN WILL DO JUST AS WELL.

Ingredients

450g/1lb plain flour

1 tsp salt

1 tsp sugar

90ml/3 fl oz milk

30g/1oz fresh yeast

60g/2oz butter or ghee

150ml/5 fl oz natural yogurt

1 large egg, beaten

2 tbsps sesame seeds
or poppy seeds

TIME Preparation takes 1¼ to
2 hours and cooking takes about
10 minutes.

VARIATION Mix crushed garlic
and freshly chopped coriander
into the yogurt before glazing the
naan breads.

1. Place the flour, salt and sugar in a large bowl, and mix together well.

2. Heat the milk until it is lukewarm, crumble in the yeast and leave for 3 to 4 minutes before stirring until the yeast is completely dissolved. Melt the butter, then leave it until it is just lukewarm.

3. Add the yeast liquid, all but 1 tbsp of the yogurt, the egg and melted butter to the flour. Mix to a soft dough, turn out onto a floured surface and knead until soft and elastic.

4. Place the dough in a clean bowl, cover and leave in a warm place for about 1 hour, until doubled in bulk.

5. Divide the dough into 8 balls, kneading them lightly then cover and leave for 10 to 15 minutes.

6. Place two ungreased baking sheets in a preheated 230°C/450°F/Gas mark 8 oven for about 10 minutes to heat through. Remove the hot baking sheets from the oven and flour them lightly.

7. Stretch or roll the balls into teardrop shapes about 15cm/6 inches long. Place on the baking sheets, brush with the reserved yogurt and sprinkle with the sesame seeds or poppy seeds.

8. Bake one sheet at a time on the top shelf of the oven for about 10 minutes, or until puffed and browned.

Serves 6

Ratatouille

THIS DELICIOUS VEGETABLE CASSEROLE FROM THE SOUTH OF FRANCE
HAS BECOME A GREAT FAVOURITE ACROSS THE WORLD.

Ingredients

75ml/5 tbsps olive oil

2 red onions, thinly sliced

2 green or red peppers,
cored and coarsely chopped

4 courgettes, thickly sliced

2 aubergines, coarsely
chopped

2 x 790g/1lb 12oz tin
peeled plum tomatoes

1 large clove garlic, crushed

2½ tsps chopped fresh basil

Salt and freshly ground
black pepper

140ml/¼ pint dry white wine

1. Heat the oil in a large saucepan, add the onion slices and fry for 5 minutes until they are soft and just beginning to brown.

2. Stir in the peppers and courgette, and cook gently for 5 minutes until they begin to soften. Remove all the vegetables from the pan and set them aside.

3. Put the chopped aubergine into the saucepan with the vegetable juices. Cook gently until it begins to brown.

4. Add the canned tomatoes, garlic and basil to the saucepan along with the sautéed vegetables, mixing well to blend in evenly. Bring to the boil, reduce the heat and simmer for 15 minutes, or until the liquid in the pan reduces and thickens.

5. Add the seasoning and wine to the pan and continue cooking for a further 15 minutes, before serving straight away, or chilling and serving cold.

COOK'S TIP If the liquid in the pan is still thin and excessive after the full cooking time, remove the vegetables and boil the juices rapidly until they have reduced and thickened.

TIME Preparation takes 20 minutes, plus 30 minutes standing time. Cooking takes about 35 minutes.

Courgettes A member of the squash family, courgettes are picked young and are smaller than many of their cousins. Most varieties are dark green in colour, although both a variegated and a yellow variety are also available. Courgette flowers are occasionally sold and these edible blossoms are delicious stuffed and baked.

Cardamom Rice

THE DELICATE FLAVOUR OF THIS INDIAN RICE DISH MAKES IT
SUITABLE FOR SERVING WITH A WHOLE HOST OF DISHES.

Ingredients

280g/10oz basmati rice

60g/2oz ghee or unsalted butter

6 green cardamoms,
split open on the top

1 tsp black cumin seeds or
caraway seeds

1 tsp salt or to taste

500ml/18 fl oz water

TIME Preparation takes 5 to 10 minutes plus time needed to soak the rice; cooking takes 20 to 25 minutes.

1. Wash the rice, soak in cold water for ½ to 1 hour and drain thoroughly.

2. Melt the ghee or butter over low heat and fry the cardamom and caraway seeds for 1 minute.

3. Add the rice, stir and fry over medium heat for 2 to 3 minutes. Adjust heat to low, stir and fry for another 2 to 3 minutes.

4. Add salt and water and mix well. Bring to the boil, cover the pan and simmer for 12 minutes, without lifting the lid.

5. Remove from the heat and leave the pot undisturbed for 6 to 8 minutes before serving.

COOK'S TIP Do not lift the lid or stir the rice during cooking. Do not stir immediately after the rice has been cooked.

Serves 4

Aubergine and Pepper Szechuan Style

AUTHENTIC SZECHUAN FOOD IS FIERY HOT. OUTSIDE CHINA,
RESTAURANTS OFTEN TONE DOWN THE TASTE FOR WESTERN PALATES.

Ingredients

Oil for frying

1 large aubergine, cubed

2 cloves garlic, crushed

2.5cm/1-inch piece root ginger,
peeled and shredded

1 onion, cubed

1 small green pepper, cored
and cut into 2.5cm/1-inch pieces

1 small red pepper, cored
and cut into 2.5cm/1-inch pieces

1 red or green chilli, cored
and cut into thin strips

120ml/4 fl oz vegetable stock

1 tsp sugar

1 tsp vinegar

Pinch of salt and freshly
ground black pepper

1 tsp cornflour

1 tbsp soy sauce

Dash of sesame oil

Oil for cooking

TIME Preparation takes about 30 minutes
and cooking takes 7 to 8 minutes.

1. Heat about 3 tbsps oil in a wok. Add the aubergine and stir-fry 4 to 5 minutes. It may be necessary to add more oil as the aubergine cooks. Remove from the wok and set aside.

2. Reheat the wok and add 2 tbsps oil. Add the garlic and root ginger and stir-fry for 1 minute. Add the onion and stir-fry for 2 minutes. Add the pepper and chilli, and stir-fry for 1 minute. Return the aubergine to the wok along with the remaining ingredients.

3. Bring to the boil, stirring constantly, and cook until the sauce thickens and clears. Serve immediately.

Aubergine *The aubergine is thought to have originated in India, from where it spread gradually to other warm regions. It is basically a large berry which can vary in shape from oblong to round, and in colour from white to deep purple. When choosing an aubergine, pick the small fruits, which have a superior flavour.*

Serves 4

Stir-fried Sticky Rice

THE CHINESE OFTEN SERVE STICKY RICE – IT NOT
ONLY HAS A LOVELY TEXTURE, BUT IT IS EASIER TO
EAT WITH CHOPSTICKS.

Ingredients

250g/9oz glutinous rice

2 tbsps vegetable oil

*2 spring onions,
chopped*

½ onion, chopped

1 slice fresh root ginger

*4 dried Chinese black
mushrooms, soaked for
15 minutes in warm water,
drained and sliced*

*Salt and freshly ground
black pepper*

TIME Preparation takes
5 minutes and cooking takes
approximately 25 minutes.

1. Wash the rice in cold water and place it in a sieve. Pour 1.3 litres/2¼ pints boiling water over the rice.

2. Heat the oil in a wok and fry the spring onions, onion and root ginger until golden brown. Add the mushrooms and continue cooking, stirring and shaking the wok frequently.

3. Add the rice and stir well. Pour over enough water to cover the rice by about 1cm/½ inch.

4. Cover and cook over a moderate heat until there is almost no liquid left. Reduce the heat once again and continue cooking until all the liquid has been absorbed – this takes about 20 minutes. Add salt and pepper to taste, remove the slice of root ginger and serve immediately.

Right: Stir-fried Sticky Rice

Serves 4

Leeks Provençal

A BASIC PROVENÇAL SAUCE OF TOMATOES, GARLIC
AND HERBS GOES WELL WITH MOST SAVOURY DISHES.
WITH LEEKS IT IS EXCEPTIONAL.

Ingredients

6 leeks, washed and trimmed

Salt

1 tbsp olive oil

2 cloves garlic, crushed

4 tomatoes, peeled, seeded
and chopped

1 tsp dried thyme

2 tbsps chopped fresh parsley

60ml/2 fl oz dry white wine

Freshly ground black pepper

Sprigs of fresh parsley
to garnish

1. Cut the leeks into 5cm/2-inch pieces
   and cook for 10 to 15 minutes in
   lightly salted, boiling water until tender.

2. Heat the oil in a small saucepan and
   fry the garlic until softened, but not
   browned. Stir in the tomatoes, herbs
   and wine, and simmer gently for
   10 minutes until the tomatoes are soft.
   Season with salt and pepper.

3. Drain the cooked leeks and place in a
   serving dish with the tomato mixture.
   Toss to mix. Serve garnished with a
   sprig of parsley.

TIME Preparation takes about
10 minutes and cooking takes
25 minutes.

Long Beans in Coconut Milk

IN THIS THAI RECIPE, THE LONG BEANS ARE LIGHTLY COOKED
AND SHOULD STILL BE SLIGHTLY CRUNCHY WHEN SERVED.

Ingredients

450g/1lb long beans

1 tbsp oil

2 stems lemongrass, sliced

2.5cm/10-inch piece galangal,
sliced into thin sticks

1 large red chilli, seeded and
chopped

280ml/½ pint thin coconut milk

Chilli 'flowers' to garnish

1. Top and tail the beans and cut into
   5cm/2-inch pieces.

2. Heat the oil in a wok and stir-fry the
   lemongrass, galangal and chilli for
   1 minute. Add the coconut milk and
   bring to the boil. Boil for 3 minutes.

3. Stir in the beans, reduce the heat and
   simmer for 6 minutes. Garnish with
   chilli 'flowers' (see below) and serve
   immediately.

TIME Preparation takes 10 minutes and
cooking takes 7 minutes.

Red Chillies *Red chillies are used extensively in
Asian cooking, both as an ingredient and as a garnish. Chilli
flowers, a popular garnish, are made by slicing the chilli from
stem to tip and soaking it in ice water until the strips
curl. As well as being used fresh, chillies are
also dried to preserve them and
intensify their flavour.*

Serves 4–6

Saag Bhaji

SPINACH ADOPTS OTHER FLAVOURS WELL. HERE, A DELICIOUS RESULT IS OBTAINED
BY SIMMERING IT IN SPICES AND THEN COMBINING IT WITH DICED, FRIED POTATOES.

Ingredients

90ml/3 fl oz cooking oil

½ tsp mustard seeds

1 tsp cumin seeds

8-10 fenugreek seeds (optional)

1 tbsp curry leaves or
1 tsp curry powder

2-3 cloves garlic, finely chopped

2-4 dried red chillies,
coarsely chopped

450g/1lb fresh leaf spinach
or 225g/8oz frozen leaf spinach,
finely chopped

1 tbsp ghee or unsalted butter

1 large potato, peeled and diced

1 large onion, finely sliced

½ tsp ground turmeric

1 tsp ground cumin

½ tsp garam masala

¼-½ tsp chilli powder

2-3 ripe tomatoes, peeled
and chopped

1 tsp salt or to taste

1. Heat 2 tbsps oil from the specified amount over medium heat and fry the mustard seeds until they pop. Add the cumin seeds, fenugreek (if using) and curry leaves or powder. Now add the garlic and chilli peppers, and fry until the garlic turns slightly brown.

2. Add the spinach, stir and mix thoroughly. Cover and simmer for 15 minutes, stirring occasionally.

3. Melt the ghee or butter over medium heat, add the potatoes and brown them. Remove from heat and set aside.

4. Heat the remaining oil over medium heat and fry the onions until well browned, about 10 minutes. Do not burn the onions or they will taste bitter.

5. Turn the heat down to minimum and add the turmeric, cumin, garam masala and chilli powder. Stir and fry for 2 to 3 minutes.

6. Add the spinach, potatoes, tomatoes and salt. Cover and simmer for 10 minutes or until the potatoes are tender, stirring occasionally. Remove from the heat and serve.

TIME Preparation takes 25 to 30 minutes
and cooking takes 50 minutes.

Serves 4

Stir-fried Chinese Leaves

CHINESE LEAF IS FLAVOURED WITH SESAME OIL AND
SOY SAUCE IN THIS TASTY DISH.

Ingredients

2 courgettes

2 tbsps vegetable oil

450g/1lb Chinese leaves,
finely shredded

1 tsp chopped garlic

1 tbsp chopped red chilli

1 tbsp soy sauce

Salt and freshly ground
pepper

Few tsps sesame oil

1. Prepare the courgettes, first topping
   and tailing them and then slicing down
   the sides, preserving a bit of the flesh
   with the peel. Slice finely.

2. Heat the oil in a wok, add the Chinese
   leaves and garlic, and stir-fry for
   2 minutes.

3. Add the courgette, chilli, soy sauce,
   salt and pepper. Continue cooking for
   3 minutes and serve hot with the
   sesame oil drizzled on top.

PREPARATION Cooked in this way, the
Chinese leaves will remain crisp. If you
prefer, cook longer for a softer texture.

VARIATION If you like hot, spicy dishes,
add chilli sauce to taste to the Chinese
leaves.

TIME Preparation takes about
10 minutes and cooking takes
5 minutes.

Right: Stir-fried Chinese Leaves

Serves 4

Turkish Pilaf

TURKEY IS FAMOUS FOR ITS APRICOTS, SULTANAS AND PISTACHIO NUTS. THIS RECIPE MAKES GOOD USE OF THEM ALL.

Ingredients

2 tbsps oil

200g/7oz long-grain rice

570ml/1 pint water

¼ tsp salt

30g/1oz split blanched almonds

30g/1oz shelled pistachio nuts

30g/1oz sultanas

30g/1oz chopped dried apricots

TIME Preparation takes 10 to 15 minutes and cooking takes about 20 minutes.

SERVING IDEA Decorate with sprigs of fresh greens, such as coriander leaves, watercress, or lamb's lettuce.

1. Heat the oil in a large saucepan over high heat. Add the rice and cook, stirring constantly with a wooden spoon, until all the grains are coated.

2. Add water and salt and cover the pan with a cloth, then with the lid. Reduce the heat to a simmer and cook for 15 minutes.

3. Meanwhile, toast the almonds in a dry, nonstick frying pan. When they start to give off their characteristic aroma (after about 5 minutes), they are ready.

4. Remove the rice from the heat; it should have absorbed all the liquid. If not, return rice to the heat, uncovered, for a few minutes to finish evaporation. Transfer rice to a large bowl and stir in the almonds, pistachios, sultanas and apricots.

5. Serve the rice heaped in a mound on a serving platter, or press it into a ring mould brushed with oil, then unmould to give the rice an attractive shape.

Serves 4–6

Potatoes with Garlic and Chillies

THESE ARE RATHER LIKE A SPICY INDIAN VERSION
OF FRENCH FRIES, BUT THEY ARE NOT DEEP-FRIED.

Ingredients

3-4 potatoes, peeled
and washed

3 tbsps cooking oil

½ tsp mustard seeds

½ tsp cumin seeds

4 cloves garlic, crushed

¼-½ tsp chilli powder

½ tsp ground turmeric

1 tsp salt or to taste

1. Cut the potatoes to the thickness of French fries, but half their length.

2. In a large nonstick or cast-iron frying pan, heat the oil over medium heat. Add the mustard seeds and cumin. When the seeds start popping, add the garlic and allow it to turn lightly brown.

3. Remove the pan from the heat and add the chilli powder and turmeric. Add the potatoes and place the pan back on heat. Stir and turn heat up to medium.

4. Add the salt, stir and mix, cover the pan, cook for 3 to 4 minutes and stir again. Continue to do this until the potatoes are cooked and lightly browned. Remove from the heat.

TIME Preparation takes 15 to 20 minutes and cooking takes 15 minutes.

VARIATION Use cauliflower, cut into small florets, instead of potato.

Potatoes *Among the most widely cultivated vegetables, the potato is one of the world's most important staples. Easily grown and highly nutritious (it contains elements such as copper and iron, vitamin C, thiamin, riboflavin and pantothenic acid, and is low in salts), it is cultivated on every continent and virtually every country has a plethora of recipes that include it.*

Makes 12

Wheat Tortillas

THESE MEXICAN UNLEAVENED FLAT BREADS ARE MADE WITH WHEAT FLOUR AND ARE
EASIER TO PREPARE THAN THE MORE AUTHENTIC CORN VARIETY.

Ingredients

450g/1lb plain flour

1 tbsp salt

90g/3oz margarine

280ml/½ pint hot water

TIME Preparation takes 20 to 25 minutes and cooking takes about 5 minutes.

COOK'S TIP Do not overcook tortillas; they must be pliable or they will crack when rolled around a filling.

1. Mix the flour and salt together in a bowl then cut in the margarine until the mixture resembles breadcrumbs. Gradually add the water to form a soft, pliable dough.

2. Knead the dough on a well-floured surface until smooth and no longer sticky. Divide the dough into 12 pieces, keeping the dough that is not being worked covered to prevent it from drying out.

3. Knead each piece into a ball, then roll out each ball into a very thin circle, using a floured rolling pin. Cut into neat rounds using a 25cm/10-inch plate as a guide.

4. Stack the tortillas as you make them, flouring each one well to prevent them from sticking together. Cover with a clean cloth.

5. Heat a heavy-based frying pan until evenly hot and carefully add a tortilla.

Cook for about 10 seconds per side. Stack and keep covered until all are cooked. Use according to your recipe.

Makes 1 Large Loaf

English Cottage Milk Loaf

BREADS WITH MILK HAVE A MUCH SOFTER CRUST THAN THOSE MADE WITH WATER.
THIS IS IDEAL FOR COTTAGE LOAVES AS IT MAKES THEM EASIER TO SLICE.

Ingredients

15g/½oz fresh yeast

430ml/¾ pint warm milk

680g/1½lbs strong plain flour

1 tsp salt

60g/2oz butter

Beaten egg to glaze

Poppy seeds

TIME Preparation takes about
2 hours and cooking takes
30 to 35 minutes.

COOK'S TIP Ensure you seal
the topknot on firmly.

1. Crumble the yeast into half the milk
and leave for 3 to 4 minutes, then stir
to completely dissolve the yeast.

2. Mix the flour and salt together, and rub
in the butter. Make a well in the centre
and pour in the yeast liquid. Mix to a
soft but manageable dough, adding as
much of the remaining milk as
necessary.

3. Turn out onto a lightly-floured surface
and knead thoroughly until smooth and
elastic. Return the dough to the bowl,
cover and leave in a warm place for
45 to 60 minutes, until doubled in bulk.

4. Knock back the dough and divide into
two, one piece being about double the
size of the other.

5. Shape the larger piece of dough into a
round loaf and place it on a floured
baking sheet. Shape the small piece into a
round and place it on top. Flour the
handle of a wooden spoon and press it
firmly through the centre of the topknot,
down to the baking sheet, to seal the two
pieces. Cover loosely and leave in a warm
place for about 30 minutes, until the loaf
is well risen.

6. Brush the loaf with beaten egg and
sprinkle some poppy seeds over the top
of the loaf. Bake in a preheated 220°C/
425°F/Gas mark 7 oven for 30 to 35
minutes, until the loaf sounds hollow
when tapped underneath. Transfer to a
wire rack to cool.

Serves 4–6

Carrot Pilau

PLAIN BOILED RICE IS TRANSFORMED INTO A COLOURFUL
AND FLAVOURSOME PILAU IN THIS AROMATIC DISH.

Ingredients

280g/10oz basmati rice,
washed and soaked in cold
water for ½ hour

500ml/18 fl oz water

1 tsp salt or to taste

1 tsp butter

2 tbsps ghee or unsalted butter

1 tsp cumin or caraway seeds

1 onion, finely sliced

2 cinnamon sticks, 5cm/2 inches
long, broken up

4 green cardamoms, split open

1 tsp garam masala or ground
mixed spice

180g/6oz carrots, coarsely grated

120g/4oz frozen peas

½ tsp salt or to taste

1. Drain the rice thoroughly and put into a saucepan with the water. Bring to the boil and stir in the salt and 1 tsp butter. Boil steadily for 1 minute.

2. Place the lid on the saucepan and simmer for 12 to 15 minutes. Do not lift the lid during cooking.

3. Remove the pan from heat and keep it covered for another 10 minutes.

4. Meanwhile, prepare the rest of the ingredients. Melt the 2 tbsps ghee over medium heat, add the cumin or caraway seeds and fry until they crackle.

5. Add the onion, cinnamon and cardamom, and fry until the onions are lightly browned, about 4 to 5 minutes, stirring frequently.

6. Add the garam masala or ground mixed spice. Stir and cook for 30 seconds. Add the carrots, peas and salt, stir and then cook for 1 to 2 minutes.

7. Now add the rice, stir and mix gently using a metal spoon or a fork as a wooden spoon or spatula will squash the grains. Remove the pan from heat and serve.

TIME Preparation takes about 15 minutes, plus time needed to soak the rice. Cooking takes 25 to 30 minutes.

Carrots *The carrot has been cultivated since about 500 BC, and over the centuries the sweet and savoury characteristics of this extremely adaptable vegetable have resulted in it being used in everything from drinks to cakes. On the health side, carrots are rich in vitamins, particularly vitamin A.*

DESSERTS

Obviously, choosing a dessert presents vegetarians with far
fewer problems than other courses, and their inclusion in a
vegetarian book may seem a little unnecessary. The choice of
desserts in this section, however, is designed to complement
our main courses without any of those hidden surprises,
such as gelatine.

As you would expect, many of the best desserts from around the
world are based on fruit. A simple fruit salad is one of the most
healthy desserts, and we have included a few variations on this
theme. These are great for everyday meals but, if something just
that little bit special is called for, try Raspberry Soufflé, Coconut
and Banana Pancakes, or Spiced Mango Fool. If it's a taste of the
exotic you crave, indulge in Vermicelli Kheer, or
a delicious Kompot.

Serves 4

Spun Fruits

OFTEN CALLED TOFFEE FRUITS, THIS CHINESE SWEET CONSISTS OF FRUIT
FRIED IN BATTER AND COATED WITH A CRISP CARAMEL GLAZE.

Ingredients

Oil for deep frying

Batter

120g/4oz plain flour, sieved

Pinch of salt

1 egg

*140ml/¼ pint water and milk,
mixed half and half*

Caramel syrup

225g/8oz sugar

3 tbsps water

1 tbsp oil

*1 large apple, peeled, cored and
cut into 5cm/2-inch chunks*

*1 banana, peeled and cut
into 2.5cm/1-inch pieces*

Ice water

1. Combine all the batter ingredients in a food processor or blender and process to blend. Pour into a bowl and dip in the prepared fruit.

2. In a heavy-based pan, combine the sugar with the water and oil, and cook over very low heat until the sugar dissolves. Bring to the boil and boil rapidly until a pale caramel colour.

3. While the sugar is dissolving, heat the oil in a wok or saucepan and fry the battered fruit, a few pieces at a time.

4. While the fruit is still hot and crisp, use chopsticks or a pair of tongs to dip the fruit into the hot caramel syrup. Stir each piece around to coat evenly.

5. Dip immediately into ice water to harden the syrup, and place each piece on a greased dish. Continue cooking all the fruit in the same way.

6. Once the caramel has hardened and the fruit has cooled, transfer to a clean serving plate.

TIME Preparation takes 25 minutes and cooking takes 10 to 15 minutes.

COOK'S TIP Watch the syrup carefully and do not allow it to become too brown, as this will give the dish a bitter taste.

Serves 6

Raspberry Soufflé

THIS RECIPE USES A VEGETABLE GELLING POWDER, GELOZONE. MANY SIMILAR PRODUCTS ARE AVAILABLE, SIMPLY FOLLOW THE INSTRUCTIONS ON THE PACKET.

Ingredients

450g/1lb raspberries (frozen raspberries, thawed, can be used)

60g/2oz icing sugar

1½ tsps Gelozone

200ml/7 fl oz water

4 eggs, separated

120g/4oz caster sugar

280ml/½ pint double cream, lightly whipped

Mint sprigs to decorate

TIME Preparation takes about 1 hour.

1. Tie a piece of lightly greased greaseproof paper around a 15cm/6-inch soufflé dish to form a collar above the rim of the dish.

2. Reserve a few of the raspberries and strain the rest through a sieve. Fold the icing sugar into the raspberry purée.

3. Add the Gelozone to the water and heat until boiling. Set aside.

4. Whip the egg yolks and sugar together over the hot water. Fold in the raspberry purée and Gelozone, and cool slightly. Fold in half the cream.

5. Whip the egg whites until stiff, then fold into the mixture with a metal spoon. Turn into the prepared soufflé dish and leave to set.

6. Remove the collar and decorate the soufflé with the cream, raspberries and mint sprigs.

Raspberries *Raspberries grow wild in rocky woodland throughout Europe and are cultivated in many other areas. The berries are ripe when they are brightly and evenly coloured, and slip easily off their hulls. Ideally, they should be used as soon as they have been picked as they spoil rapidly.*

Serves 4

Coconut and Banana Pancakes

THIS UNUSUAL DESSERT FROM THAILAND
CAN BE SERVED WARM OR COLD.

Ingredients

120g/4oz rice flour

Pinch of salt

2 eggs

280ml/½ pint thin coconut milk

Green food colouring (optional)

30g/1oz shredded or desiccated coconut

Oil for frying

Filling

2 tbsps lime juice

Grated rind of ½ lime

1 tsp sugar

1 tbsp shredded or desiccated coconut

2 bananas

1. Place the flour and the salt in a mixing bowl and make a well in the centre. Drop the eggs and a little of the coconut milk into the well.

2. Using a wooden spoon, beat well, slowly incorporating the flour until you have a smooth, thick paste.

3. Gradually beat in the remaining coconut milk. Stir in a few drops of food colouring, if using. Allow to stand for 20 minutes.

4. Meanwhile, make the filling. Mix together the lime juice, rind, sugar and 1 tbsp coconut. Slice the bananas and toss them in the mixture.

5. Stir the 2 tbsps coconut into the pancake batter. Heat a little oil in an 20cm/8-inch heavy-based frying pan. Pour off the excess and spoon in about 4 tbsps of the batter. Swirl to coat the pan. Cook for about 1 minute, or until the underside is golden.

6. Flip or toss the pancake over and cook the other side. Slide the pancake out of the pan and keep warm. Repeat until all the batter is used. Fill the pancakes with the banana mixture and serve immediately.

SERVING IDEA Fold the pancakes into quarters and spoon some filling inside, or divide filling between the pancakes and roll up.

TIME Preparation takes 15 minutes, plus 20 minutes standing time. Cooking takes 15 minutes.

Bananas *Alexander the Great is known to have come across bananas on his travels to India and subsequently, thanks to explorers and conquerors, the banana plant spread throughout the tropical world. In Europe and temperate America, however, they remained virtually unknown until the 1890s, when the first refrigerated ships were able to transport them over long distances.*

Serves 6–8

Key Lime Pie

THE FLORIDA KEYS ARE HOME TO THIS DELIGHTFULLY
SHARP AND REFRESHING DESSERT.

Ingredients

Crust

225g/8oz digestive biscuit crumbs

120g/4oz sugar

120g/4oz butter or
margarine, melted

Filling

2 eggs

430g/15oz sweetened
condensed milk

120ml/4 fl oz lime juice

¼ tsp salt

Topping

225ml/8 fl oz soured cream

60g/2oz sugar

⅛ tsp salt

Garnish

Digestive biscuit crumbs

Grated lime rind

TIME Preparation takes about
25 minutes and cooking takes
25 minutes.

1. First prepare the base by blending together the crust ingredients. Press the mixture firmly into a 23cm/9-inch pie dish or flan ring with removable base. Bake in a preheated 180°C/350°F/Gas mark 4 oven for 10 minutes.

2. To prepare the filling, beat the eggs and milk together, and add the lime juice and salt. Pour the filling into the prepared crust and return the pie to the oven for 10 minutes, or until set.

3. Meanwhile, prepare the topping by combining the soured cream, sugar and salt. When the filling has set, spread the topping over the pie. Bake at 220°C/ 425°F/ Gas mark 7 for 5 minutes to set the topping. Garnish with cracker crumbs and lime rind, and serve cold.

Serves 6 – 8

Cassata

NO SWEET SELECTION IS COMPLETE WITHOUT ICE CREAM.
THE ITALIAN KIND IS RICH, CREAMY AND JUSTLY FAMOUS.

Ingredients

Almond layer

2 eggs, separated

60g/2oz icing sugar

140ml/¼ pint double cream

½ tsp almond essence

Chocolate layer

2 eggs, separated

60g/2oz icing sugar

140ml/¼ pint double cream

60g/2oz plain chocolate

2 tbsps cocoa powder

1½ tbsps water

Fruit layer

280ml/½ pint double cream

2 tbsps maraschino or light rum

1 egg white

60g/2oz icing sugar

60g/2oz glacé fruit

30g/1oz shelled, chopped pistachios

1. To prepare the almond layer, beat the egg whites until stiff peaks form, gradually beating in the icing sugar a spoonful at a time. Lightly beat the egg yolks and fold in the whites.

2. Whip the cream with the almond essence until soft peaks form, then fold into the egg mixture. Lightly oil an 20cm/8-inch round cake tin. Pour in the almond layer mixture and smooth over the top. Cover with plastic wrap and freeze until firm.

3. To prepare the chocolate layer, beat the egg whites until stiff peaks form, gradually beating in the icing sugar a spoonful at a time. Whip the cream until soft, then fold into the egg white mixture. Melt the chocolate in the top of a double boiler over simmering water. Remove it from the heat and stir in the egg yolks. Combine the cocoa and water and add to the chocolate mixture. Leave to cool and then fold into the egg white mixture. Spoon the chocolate layer over the almond layer and return, covered, to the freezer.

4. To make the rum fruit layer, whip the cream until soft peaks form. Whip the egg white until about the same consistency as cream. Gradually add the icing sugar, beating well after each addition. Combine the two mixtures and fold in the rum, fruit and nuts. Spread this mixture over the chocolate layer, cover and freeze until firm.

5. To serve, loosen the cassata from around the edges of the pan with a small knife. Place a hot cloth around the pan for a few seconds to help loosen. Turn out onto a serving plate and cut into wedges to serve.

TIME Preparation takes several hours, so that one ice cream layer can freeze before another is added.

Serves 6

Tarte Tatin

THIS CLASSIC FRENCH 'UPSIDE-DOWN' TART IS SAID
TO HAVE BEEN INVENTED BY ACCIDENT BY THE TWO
SISTERS TATIN IN THEIR HOTEL IN THE LOIRE.

Ingredients

90g/3oz butter

180g/6oz sugar

1kg/2¼lbs apples, peeled,
halved and cored

450g/1lb flaky pastry (use puff if
flaky is unavailable)

3 tbsps double cream

TIME Preparation takes about
15 minutes and cooking takes
30 minutes.

1. Dot the base of a medium pie dish
   with the butter and sprinkle with half
   the sugar.

2. Place the apple halves, rounded side
   down, on to the butter and sugar, and
   sprinkle over the remaining sugar.

3. Roll the pastry out into a round just
   slightly larger than the bottom of the
   pan. Place the pastry round over the
   apples, tucking it down at the edges.

4. Bake in a preheated 230°C/450°F/Gas
   mark 8 oven for about 30 minutes.
   Remove from the oven when cooked
   and turn out immediately onto a
   serving plate.

5. Whip the cream and serve in a small
   bowl for guests to help themselves.

Apples *Of all the fruits that grow in the
temperate world, the apple is the undoubted king.
The Ancient Egyptians cultivated apple trees and
the Greeks and Romans knew them well. By the end of the
4th century AD, there were 37 varieties on record. From then on,
wherever Western civilisation went, apples went too.*

Serves 6

Vermicelli Kheer

IN THIS POPULAR INDIAN DESSERT, THE VERMICELLI
IS LIGHTLY FRIED IN GHEE, THEN SIMMERED IN MILK
AND SPICES TO MAKE A RICH AND CREAMY DISH.

Ingredients

2 tbsps ghee or unsalted butter

280g/10oz plain vermicelli

30g/1oz sultanas

30g/1oz almonds, blanched and
slivered

570ml/1 pint full cream milk

60g/2oz sugar

1 tbsp ground almonds

½ tsp ground cardamom

½ tsp ground cinnamon

1 tbsp rose water, or 5-6 drops
of other flavourings such as
vanilla or almond

1. Melt the ghee or butter over low heat in a large pan and add the vermicelli, sultanas and slivered almonds. Stir and fry for 2 to 3 minutes, until the vermicelli is golden brown.

2. Add the milk, sugar and ground almonds, bring to the boil and simmer gently for 20 minutes, stirring frequently.

3. Stir in the ground cardamom and cinnamon, and remove the pan from the heat.

4. Allow the kheer to cool slightly and stir in the rose water or other flavouring before serving.

TIME Preparation takes 10 minutes and cooking takes 20 to 25 minutes.

Left: Tarte Tatin

Serves 6–8

Jamaican Mousse Cake

RUM, CHOCOLATE AND BANANAS – TRUE TASTES OF THE CARIBBEAN –
ARE COMBINED IN THIS ENTICING DESSERT.

Ingredients

180g/6oz plain chocolate

3 tbsps dark rum

280ml/½ pint double cream

2 large bananas, peeled
and mashed until smooth

1 tbsp light muscovado sugar

1 tbsp strong black coffee

3 eggs, separated

Chocolate curls to decorate

TIME Preparation takes about
30 minutes, plus chilling.

1. Break the chocolate into cubes and
place in a bowl over a pan of hot water,
or the top of a bain marie, to melt.
Once melted, stir in the rum and half of
the cream, beating well until smooth.

2. Put the mashed bananas, sugar and
coffee in a large bowl, and beat until well
combined. Add the egg yolks and mix
well. Continue beating while adding all
the chocolate mixture.

3. Beat the egg whites until stiff and
forming peaks, then fold into the banana
mixture.

4. Spoon the mixture into a lightly greased
20cm/8-inch springform cake tin. Chill
for at least 2 hours, or until completely
set and firm.

5. Loosen the sides of the cake with a
warm knife, then remove the sides of
the pan. Carefully slide the cake off the
base of the tin on to a serving plate.

6. Whip the remaining cream and decorate
the cake with swirls of cream and
chocolate curls.

Serves 6–8

Spiced Mango Fool

IN INDIA, MANGO IS CONSIDERED TO BE THE KING OF ALL FRUITS. THE TASTE OF THIS TROPICAL FRUIT IS A LITTLE LIKE A PEACH, BUT MUCH MORE EXOTIC.

Ingredients

2 tbsps milk

¼ tsp saffron strands

180ml/6 fl oz evaporated milk

60g/2oz sugar

1 level tbsp fine semolina

2 heaped tbsps ground almonds

1 tsp ground cardamom

450g/1lb mango pulp, or
2 x 425g/15oz cans of mangoes,
drained and puréed

250ml/9 fl oz unflavoured
fromage frais

TIME Preparation takes 10 minutes and cooking takes 10 to 15 minutes.

1. Put the milk into a small saucepan and bring to the boil. Stir in the saffron strands, remove from the heat, cover the pan and set aside.

2. Put the evaporated milk and sugar into a separate saucepan and place over a low heat. When the milk begins to bubble, sprinkle the semolina over and stir until well blended.

3. Add the ground almonds, stir and cook until the mixture thickens – about 5 to 6 minutes.

4. Stir in the ground cardamom and remove from the heat. Allow this to cool completely, then gradually beat in the mango pulp, making sure there are no lumps.

5. In a large mixing bowl, beat the fromage frais with a fork. Gradually beat in the evaporated milk and mango mixture.

6. Stir in the saffron milk, along with all the strands. Mix well. Put the mango fool in a serving dish and chill for 2 to 3 hours before serving.

Strawberries *Today's large, succulent strawberries would have been a revelation to our ancestors, whose wild strawberries were much smaller. Big is not necessarily beautiful, however. One of the most flavoursome varieties is the Alpine strawberry, a miniature plant that produces fruit throughout the summer.*

Serves 4

Figs with Currants and Orange

FRUIT IS THE MOST POPULAR DESSERT IN GREECE,
AND FRESH FIGS ARE A FAVOURITE CHOICE.

Ingredients

4 fresh figs

*Small bunches of fresh
redcurrants*

6 oranges

1 tsp orange flower water

TIME Preparation takes about
15 minutes, plus chilling time.

1. Cut the stalks off the tops of the figs,
   but do not peel them. Cut the figs in
   quarters, but do not cut completely
   through the base. Open the figs out like
   flowers and stand them on their bases
   on serving dishes.

2. Arrange small bunches of redcurrants
   on the figs. Squeeze the juice from two
   of the oranges. Peel and segment the
   other four and arrange segments around
   each fig.

3. Mix the orange juice mixed with the
   orange flower water and pour over the
   figs. Chill before serving.

SERVING IDEA Yogurt and honey may
be served as an accompaniment.

Orange *China is thought to be the home of the sweet
orange, which first found its way across Europe with the Romans.
Its spread did not end there, however, and today there are huge
orange groves in North Africa, Israel, Florida and California.*

Serves 4

Mexican Chocolate Flan

A FLAN IN MEXICO IS A MOULDED CUSTARD WITH A CARAMEL SAUCE.
CHOCOLATE AND CINNAMON ARE A FAVOURITE FLAVOUR COMBINATION.

Ingredients

120g/4oz sugar

2 tbsps water

Juice of ½ a lemon

280ml/½ pint milk

60g/2oz plain chocolate

1 cinnamon stick

2 whole eggs

2 egg yolks

60g/2oz sugar

1. Combine the 120g/4oz sugar with the water and lemon juice in a small, heavy-based saucepan.

2. Cook over gentle heat until the sugar starts to dissolve. Swirl the pan from time to time, but do not stir.

3. Once the sugar dissolves, bring the syrup to the boil and cook until golden brown.

4. While preparing the syrup, heat 4 ramekins in a 180°C/350°F/Gas mark 4 oven. When the syrup is ready, pour into the ramekins and swirl to coat the sides and base evenly. Leave to cool at room temperature.

5. Chop the chocolate into small pieces and heat with the milk and cinnamon stick, stirring occasionally to help the chocolate dissolve.

6. Whip the whole eggs and the extra yolks together with the remaining sugar until slightly frothy. Gradually beat in the chocolate milk. Remove the cinnamon stick.

7. Pour the chocolate custard carefully into the ramekins and place them in a roasting pan of hand-hot water.

8. Place the roasting pan in the oven and bake the custards until just slightly wobbly in the centre, about 20 to 30 minutes. Cool at room temperature and refrigerate for several hours, or overnight, before serving. Loosen the custards carefully from the sides of the dishes and invert onto serving plates. Shake to allow the custards to drop out.

COOK'S TIP Do not allow the custard to over-cook or it will form a tough skin on top. If the oven temperature is too high, it will cause the custard to boil and spoil the texture.

TIME Preparation takes about 30 minutes and cooking takes 35 to 40 minutes.

Serves 6

Caribbean Fruit Salad

THIS FRUIT SALAD IS MADE FROM A REFRESHING MIXTURE OF TROPICAL FRUITS,
ALL OF WHICH ARE NOW EASILY AVAILABLE IN MOST SUPERMARKETS.

Ingredients

½ cantaloupe or honeydew
melon, seeds removed

½ small pineapple

2 oranges

120g/4oz fresh strawberries,
halved

1 mango, peeled and sliced

225g/8oz watermelon,
peeled and cubed

120g/4oz guava, peeled
and cubed

120g/4oz caster sugar

140ml/¼ pint white wine

Grated rind and juice of 1 lemon

TIME Preparation takes about
45 minutes and cooking takes
about 3 minutes.

PREPARATION It is unnecessary
to remove the pips from the
watermelon unless you
particularly dislike them.

1. Using a melon baller or teaspoon,
scoop out small balls from the
cantaloupe or honeydew melon.

2. Cut the piece of pineapple in half
lengthways and carefully peel away the
outer skin. Remove any eyes left in the
outside edge of the pineapple using a
potato peeler. Cut away the core from
the pineapple with a serrated knife and
slice the flesh thinly. Put the slices of
pineapple into a large bowl along with
the melon rounds.

3. Peel the oranges using a serrated knife.
Take care to remove all the white parts,
as they will flavour the fruit salad. Cut
the orange into segments, carefully
removing the inner membrane from the
segments as you slice.

4. Add the orange segments to the bowl
along with the strawberries, mango,
watermelon and guava.

5. Put the sugar, wine, lemon juice and
rind into a small saucepan and warm
through gently, stirring all the time
until the sugar has dissolved – do not
let it boil. Set aside to cool.

6. Put the syrup into the bowl along with
the fruit and mix thoroughly. Chill the
fruit salad completely before serving.

Serves 6

Kompot

THIS CLASSIC MIDDLE EASTERN DISH IS EASY TO PREPARE
AND CAN BE MADE WELL IN ADVANCE.

Ingredients

225g/8oz dried prunes

225g/8oz dried apricots

120g/4oz dried figs

120g/4oz raisins

120g/4oz blanched almonds

60g/2oz pinenuts

1 tsp cinnamon

¼ tsp nutmeg

120g/4oz brown sugar

1 tbsp culinary rose water

Juice and zest of 1 orange

1. Stone the prunes if necessary and chop coarsely.

2. Halve the apricots and quarter the figs.

3. Place the fruits in a large bowl and add the rest of the ingredients. Cover with cold water.

4. Stir well and keep in a cool place for 1 to 2 days, stirring a couple of times each day. Mix again before serving.

TIME Preparation takes 15 minutes. Standing time is 1 to 2 days.

SERVING IDEA Serve with yogurt or cream.

COOK'S TIP After 24 hours the liquid in which the Kompot is soaking will become very thick and syrupy. If you need to add more liquid, add a little orange juice.

VARIATION Other dried fruits may be used in the same quantities. Pistachio nuts can be substituted for the blanched almonds.

Melon *Melons are gourds, the sweetest and most succulent members of the family that embraces cucumbers, marrows, pumpkins and watermelons. Wherever they originated (the experts are undecided between Asia and Africa), it is certain they have been eaten and enjoyed by man for over 4,000 years.*

Index